Machine
APPLIQUÉ
A SAMPLER OF TECHNIQUES

SUE NICKELS

American Quilter's Society
P. O. Box 3290 • Paducah, KY 42002-3290
www.AQSquilt.com

Located in Paducah, Kentucky, the American Quilter's Society (AQS) is dedicated to promoting the accomplishments of today's quilters. Through its publications and events, AQS strives to honor today's quiltmakers and their work and to inspire future creativity and innovation in quiltmaking.

EDITOR: Shelley L. Hawkins
GRAPHIC DESIGN: Lisa M. Clark
COVER DESIGN: Michael Buckingham
PHOTOGRAPHY: Charles R. Lynch

Library of Congress Cataloging-in-Publication Data
Nickels, Sue.
     Machine appliqué : a sampler of techniques / Sue Nickels.
          p.cm.
     Includes bibliographical references.
     ISBN 1-57432-778-X
     1. Machine appliqué. 2. Machine appliqué–Patterns. 3. Quilts. I. American Quilter's Society. II. Title.
     TT779 .N53 2001
     746.46–dc21

                         2001001630

Additional copies of this book may be ordered from the American Quilter's Society, PO Box 3290, Paducah, KY 42002-3290, or online at www.AQSquilt.com.

Copyright © 2001, Sue Nickels

All rights reserved. No part of this book may be reproduced, stored in any retrieval system, or transmitted in any form, or by any means including but not limited to electronic, mechanical, photocopy, recording, or otherwise, without the written consent of the author and publisher. Patterns may be copied for personal use only.

Dedication

To my sister, Pat

Thank you for your constant support of my quilting, teaching, and all other aspects of my life. It's wonderful to have a sister who is a great quilter and a great friend. Remember, "All You Need Is Love!"

Love,
Sue

Susie and Patty, 1958

Acknowledgments

I would like to acknowledge the following people who have helped me throughout the process of writing this book. I could not have done it without their support.

To my patient editor, Shelley Hawkins: thank you so much for kindly answering all my questions and having faith in my abilities. Also, many thanks to editor Barbara Smith.

To the American Quilter's Society family: I am forever grateful to you for your support and encouragement of quiltmakers everywhere!

To Bernina of America: thank you for the generous use of my Bernina 170 QE sewing machine. Special thanks to Jane Garrison!

To my sister, Pat Holly: thank you for proofreading my manuscript. You are TOO good!

To my family: Jessi, for your graphic design assistance on my patterns and proofreading my manuscript; Ashley, for your computer assistance; and Tim, for your support while working on this major project!

To my good friend, Gwen Marston: thank you for your guidance and consultations on the project and for the use of your grandmother's doll quilt.

To a talented group of quilting friends: Nancy Chizek, Mary Ann Fielder, Sue Holdaway-Heys, Pat Holly, Barb Kilbourn, Ruth LaCoe, and Carol Spaly. I appreciate the quilts you have made with my patterns for the book. You are all great friends; thank you so much!

Contents

Introduction

The focus of this book is on machine appliqué techniques, using a variety of patterns. Three types of machine appliqué are explored. Choose your favorite technique for the patterns in this book.

I began quilting using all hand techniques and gradually turned to machine techniques. In 1978, I took my first quilt class at a local shop. My first quilt was a hand-pieced and hand-quilted Grandmother's Flower Garden pattern. The next few years were spent exploring hand-piecing techniques. My first quilt accepted in a national show was exhibited at the American Quilter's Society (AQS) Show in 1988, an intricately pieced sampler quilt, completely hand stitched. Although the process was enjoyable and provided a solid foundation for my quiltmaking, it took years to complete my quilt. I named the quilt WISHFUL THINKING because I kept wishing to be finished.

I thought one way to get quilts done a little more quickly might be to make smaller quilts. WILD ROSES AT GRANDMA'S, page 9, was made in 1988, my first appliqué quilt, again with hand techniques. I fell in love with appliqué and appliqué quilts. This quilt had a simple vine with appliquéd roses on the border to symbolize my grandmother's wild roses. The quilt was exhibited at the AQS Show in 1990.

It was also in 1990 that I discovered the movement toward machine techniques in quiltmaking. I started learning machine-piecing techniques and then explored machine-quilting techniques in depth. Having sewn on the machine as a young girl, I was an experienced seamstress. It did not take long to discover how much fun it was to use the sewing machine to make quilts.

Invisible appliqué, the first technique shown in this book, was used to make my first machine-appliquéd quilt. LET IT GROW, page 10, was exhibited nationally by the International Quilt Association in 1993. With my first machine appliqué quilts, I wanted the results to look like hand appliqué, and the invisible technique achieved that goal. My quilt ALBERTA ROSE, page 11, was also made by using the invisible tech-

nique. This quilt, inspired by an antique four-block Whig Rose quilt, was exhibited in the 1993 AQS Show, and won an honorable mention. The quilt combines my love of antique quilts, unusual color schemes, and machine techniques.

My exploration with machine appliqué continued. Although happy with the invisible method, I wanted to research other techniques of machine appliqué. Becoming comfortable using the sewing machine for quilting, I did not mind if the machine stitching showed on the quilts. As usual, I viewed antique quilts for inspiration, and the look of the blanket stitch was very appealing (see BLANKET STITCHED BUTTERFLY QUILT, page 12).

Template and starch appliqué, the second technique shown in this book, features blanket stitching with black or dark thread. This gives a decorative look similar to the antique quilts that inspired me. My quilt SEPTEMBER ROSE AND BUD, page 13, was made using this technique. An important factor for this technique is having a sewing machine with a nice blanket stitch. The success of the first two techniques also comes from the type of appliqué block used. Blocks that have fairly easy-to-use appliqué pieces, large enough to turn the seam allowances, work best. Because a seam allowance is used, preparation is the most time-consuming part of the process.

Raw-edge fusible appliqué, the third technique, was developed for several reasons. The new blocks I was interested in making were more complicated, with several small pieces. It seemed overwhelming to use a technique that had an allowance to turn. I had seen raw-edge techniques used for machine appliqué, mostly on clothing, and thought they were not very quilt-like. Using a fusible web made the appliqué pieces stiff. The satin stitch on the edge of the appliqué piece also felt stiff. I soon discovered that the new fusible webs were more lightweight. Also, by cutting away most of the fusible web and having the web along only the edge of the appliqué, a more desirable result was created. I prefer using a blanket stitch instead of a satin stitch because the edge created is much softer and appealing.

My sister and I used a combination of techniques to create BLACKBIRDS FLY, page 14, which won third place in the 1996 AQS Show Group Category. The starch and template method was used on my floral blocks, while Pat used the raw-edge fusible method on her blackbird blocks. The blocks had small pieces, so the raw-edge technique was great. From that point on, we have used the technique often with great success. LE PANIER DE FLEURS, displayed at the AQS 2000 Quilt Exhibition in Nashville, Tennessee, employs the raw-edge fusible method and is completely machine appliquéd. It has only minimal piecing, with small seams in the borders, and features a center basket medallion with a vine and leaf border. All edges have scallops that are appliquéd without piecing.

It has taken a while to come to this point with my machine appliqué, but it has been a pleasurable journey. I like all my appliqué quilts, whichever technique was used, from my first hand-appliquéd project to my most recent completely machine-appliquéd quilt.

All three techniques are wonderful options. By explaining why I use each technique, you may be able to determine which is best for your specific project. The whole process has been an evolution for me. I use the raw-edge method the most right now, but only because I am appliquéing more intricate blocks. The invisible method is the most popular when I teach the techniques because it is so easy to do. It has a fantastic finished result and a very quilt-like look. The template and starch method is also popular and provides a folk look.

I still love hand appliqué and admire all the beautiful hand-appliquéd quilts. Starting by hand gave me a wonderful foundation for my quilting. I love my sewing machine and like using it for my quilting. There is room in the quilt world for all types. One technique is not better than another. All techniques, as long as they are well-done, can be admired and appreciated.

I have been teaching machine quilting and machine appliqué for more than 10 years and have taught locally, nationally, and internationally. In the fall of 1999, I had the pleasure of traveling to England with my sister to teach machine appliqué techniques to a wonderful group of quilters. Whether it is teaching friends at my local guild, students at quilt conferences around the country, or new friends in far-away locations, sharing my skills is the most enjoyable part of my quilt-making career. I hope you enjoy the three techniques presented and are inspired by the patterns to create your own beautiful machine-

WILD ROSES AT GRANDMA'S – 44" x 52".
Hand pieced, appliquéd, and quilted by the author in memory of her grandmother, Amanda Lincoln
Townsley. This quilt was exhibited at the AQS Show in 1990.

LET IT GROW – 70" x 70".
Machine pieced, appliquéd, and quilted by the author. Two patterns from the SIMPLE APPLIQUÉ SAMPLER were used in this quilt – the Double Rose and the Tulip and Heart. The invisible appliqué method was used.

Alberta Rose – 85" x 85".
Machine pieced, appliquéd, and quilted by the author. This quilt received an honorable mention at the AQS Show in 1993. It is a four-block Whig Rose design inspired by an antique Whig Rose quilt. The invisible appliqué method was used.

BLANKET STITCHED BUTTERFLY QUILT – 18" x 19".

This is a hand-stitched doll quilt made by Gwen Marston's grandmother, Nancy Belle Smith Deardorff, when she was a young girl. It is a good example of the hand blanket stitch that inspired the machine technique shown in this book.

SEPTEMBER ROSE AND BUD – *47" x 47".*
Machine pieced, appliquéd, and quilted by the author. The Rose of Sharon pattern from the CLASSIC APPLIQUÉ
SAMPLER was used in this quilt. The template and starch method was used for this project.

Photo by Lawrence Dikeman

BLACKBIRDS FLY – 90" x 90".

Machine pieced, appliquéd, and quilted by the author and Pat Holly. This quilt has received several awards, including third place in the Group Category at the 1996 AQS Show. The design was inspired by an antique folk-style quilt. It was machine appliquéd, using the template and starch method for the floral blocks and the raw-edge fusible method for the blackbird blocks.

LE PANIER DE FLEURS (THE FLOWER BASKET) – 67" x 78".
This quilt was machine appliquéd and quilted by the author. It was selected as part of the AQS 2000 Quilt Exhibition in Nashville, Tennessee, winning third place. It is my tribute to all the great appliqué quilts that have inspired me. This quilt was completely machine appliquéd, with few pieced seams in the borders. The raw-edge fusible method was used.

Section One:

Getting Started

I teach machine appliqué in various formats, but the most popular is my "Machine Appliqué: A Sampler of Techniques" class. In this class, the student is taught all three techniques using a simple rose or tulip pattern. The student can then decide which technique she likes the best. This approach might work well while learning the techniques in this book. Find a pattern you like in the SIMPLE APPLIQUÉ SAMPLER and repeat it three times, using each technique. You can compare the results and find what you like and don't like about each.

The more you do the techniques, the easier they become. Do not be discouraged with a technique too early, because each one takes practice. My preferences about each technique are indicated, as well as why I use one rather than another. However, I like all three and use them frequently. A few alternatives to the methods are covered for those who desire other options. However, using the preparation methods with the stitching choices described for each technique is recommended.

Patterns are given for three quilts. The first is called SIMPLE APPLIQUÉ SAMPLER (pgs. 52–66) because the patterns are easy. This is a good project for a beginner. All three techniques have been used in this quilt, making it a true sampler of techniques and patterns.

The second quilt is called CLASSIC APPLIQUÉ SAMPLER (pgs. 67–85) because classic appliqué patterns were my inspiration for the design. These patterns are intermediate level. They are very manageable patterns, except they have more pieces than the SIMPLE APPLIQUÉ SAMPLER. The starch and template and raw-edge fusible methods were used for these blocks. The invisible machine appliqué method could also be used.

The third quilt is called FOLK GARDEN APPLIQUÉ SAMPLER (pgs. 86–102). It has the most pieces with more intricate designs. These patterns are for a more advanced quilter. The raw-edge fusible method was used for these blocks because of the many small pieces.

To use the patterns in the book, follow the specific directions given in the pattern sections. The appliqué patterns can be traced directly from the full-sized patterns. Keep track of how many individual appliqué pieces are needed from a particular drawing and use the full-sized drawings for placement of these pieces on the background. The SIMPLE APPLIQUÉ SAMPLER blocks are small enough to have the full-size pattern presented on one page. The CLASSIC APPLIQUÉ SAMPLER and FOLK GARDEN APPLIQUÉ SAMPLER blocks are too big for one page. A half or a quarter of each block is shown on a page.

Basic finishing instructions are provided for each quilt at the end of each pattern section. This is not a piecing book, so it assumes basic quiltmaking knowledge. Refer to the many great books available on piecing and quilting for help on these subjects.

Whatever your quilting experience, I hope you find a project that is appealing and a technique you like. The Gallery, (pgs. 103–109), contains projects that use the patterns in this book in different ways. Feel free to make your quilt project as unique as you like.

Close-up of SPRING'S HERALD by Mary Ann Fielder.

Preparation Supplies

A good understanding of supplies is essential for success in quilting projects. Refer to the Sources section, page 110, for a list of the products I prefer.

COTTON SWAB OR PAINTBRUSH: Used to apply liquid starch to the turned seam allowance for the template and starch method.

FREEZER PAPER: Used to make paper patterns for the invisible machine appliqué method. All brands are equal. You will want to regularly use fresh freezer paper because, as the paper ages, it does not stick to the fabric as well. Freezer paper has a dull side and a shiny side. The designs should be drawn on the dull side and the shiny side ironed onto the fabric.

GLUE STICK: Used to glue the turned seam allowance for the invisible machine appliqué method. A fabric glue stick is preferred and available at quilt shops. Any glue stick may be used as long as it is water soluble. Store the glue stick in a zipper bag and keep it in the refrigerator. This will help the glue stay firm and keep it from drying out.

HEAT-RESISTANT TEMPLATE PLASTIC: Used to make templates for the template and starch method. Use a sharp lead pencil to draw on template plastic. Cut with paper scissors.

IRON: A good iron is essential for machine appliqué. The iron should have a flat surface with no rounded edges on the plate.

IRONING BOARD: The ironing board should have a hard surface. I made an ironing board from a flat piece of wood (11" x 18") and covered it with cotton batting and two layers of muslin. I pulled the muslin around the edge and stapled it on the back, with a staple gun.

NAIL FILE: Used in the template and starch method to smooth rough edges on the plastic templates.

PAPER-BACKED FUSIBLE WEB: Used for the raw-edge fusible method. This is a heat-activated web for adhering appliqué fabric to the background. Use a lightweight web that does not separate easily from the paper backing before heat is applied. Store fusible web flat in plastic. Careful handling will help keep the web from separating from the paper. Do not fold it or roll it tightly.

PENCILS: A sharp lead pencil is used to draw appliqué patterns on freezer paper, template plastic, and paper-backed fusible web. A fabric marking pencil is used to mark on the fabric.

SCISSORS: Paper and fabric scissors are needed.

SPRAY STARCH: Used to secure the turned seam allowance for the template and starch method. Spray the liquid in a cup and use a cotton swab to apply. Spray starch is also used as a stabilizer for background fabric. All brands are equal; however, a regular-weight starch is preferred.

STRAIGHT PINS: Used for holding appliqué pieces in place on the background. The invisible method requires long straight pins with large heads. They are easy to attach and remove. The template and starch method needs small appliqué pins to hold pieces in place on the background. These can be ironed over easily, which is necessary for this technique.

TRACING PAPER: Used for making full-size patterns. Full-size patterns may be drawn on tracing paper with a permanent marker. For asymmetrical designs, the drawing can be turned over for tracing from the reverse side (for the invisible appliqué and raw-edge fusible methods).

TWEEZERS: Used in the invisible appliqué method to remove freezer paper from sharp points.

Sewing Supplies

OPEN-TOED APPLIQUÉ FOOT: This foot is necessary for machine appliqué. It looks like a regular foot without the bar in front. It can be described as the letter "H" when looked at from above (Fig. 1–1).

SELF-THREADING NEEDLE: This needle can be used for burying the thread ends (Fig. 1–2). It is my favorite notion and stays by my machine at all times. There is a small opening at the top of the needle that allows the thread to pop into the eye, saving the time that would be used in threading the eye of a needle.

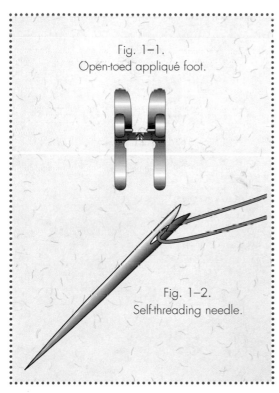

Fig. 1–1.
Open-toed appliqué foot.

Fig. 1–2.
Self-threading needle.

SEWING MACHINE: Use a good-quality sewing machine for machine appliqué. Provide yearly maintenance and keep the machine clean and oiled. The blind hem, blanket, zigzag, and straight stitches will be used. If your machine does not have some of these stitches, variations are presented. It is helpful to have a needle-down, a variable needle position option, and a presser-foot knee lift. These are not mandatory, but they are helpful for machine appliqué.

SEWING MACHINE NEEDLES: The needle size depends on the thickness of the thread used.

Thread Weight	Needle Size
Transparent nylon thread	70/10
50-weight cotton thread	80/12
30-weight cotton thread	90/14

STILETTO: Used for the template and starch method. This sharp-pointed device is used to hold the appliqué piece down when stitching so it does not curl. A long straight pin can be used instead.

Thread

COTTON THREAD (30-WEIGHT): Used for the template and starch and raw-edge fusible methods.

COTTON THREAD (50-WEIGHT): Used for the template and starch and raw-edge fusible methods. Use the best quality of thread available. Black or dark thread should be used for the template and starch method. Use a thread color that matches the appliqué fabric for the raw-edge fusible method, although a contrasting color of thread can be used for a decorative look. Do a test sample when choosing a contrasting thread color. It may look different from what you had planned.

COTTON THREAD (60-WEIGHT): Used for the invisible appliqué method. This fine embroidery thread is wound on the bobbin. The fine thread helps when using a short stitch length because a heavier thread would build up.

TRANSPARENT NYLON THREAD (.004 WEIGHT): Used for the invisible appliqué method. Nylon thread can be fussy if not threaded correctly. It comes on a heavy plastic spool and needs to be placed off the machine or the top tension will be too tight. Set the spool behind the machine and thread it through an auxiliary device. It is helpful to put an empty bobbin on the regular spool holder. Thread the nylon thread through the hole in the bobbin, then continue to

thread the machine as usual (Fig. 1–3). Thread comes off the spool without any tension. A safety pin taped to the back of the machine may also be used as an auxiliary device.

Transparent nylon thread is slightly heat sensitive. Use care when ironing.

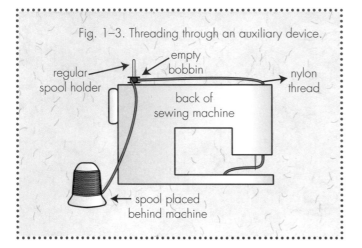

Fig. 1–3. Threading through an auxiliary device.

empty bobbin

regular spool holder

nylon thread

back of sewing machine

spool placed behind machine

Fabric

I have used only 100% cotton fabric for the machine appliqué projects in this book. Fabric with other fiber content may have varied results. Test fabrics to make sure the colors will not run or bleed onto other fabrics before using them in your appliqué blocks. Pre-wash cotton fabrics before using them in machine appliqué projects. The reaction of some of the products is slightly different if the sizing is still in the fabric.

Fabric selection is very personal. Consider the desired look for each project before selecting fabric – is it country or contemporary, for example. Choose background fabric carefully because this is the largest amount of fabric in the quilt. I usually use a solid or small tone-on-tone print. You can also use different background fabric throughout the quilt.

Choose a wide variety of fabrics for the appliqué pieces. You can vary the scale, choosing small- and large-scale prints. Most of the patterns in this book

have small pieces, so small amounts of fabric work well. I do a lot of auditioning of fabric throughout the process. Sometimes it is difficult to determine if a fabric will work until it has been cut out and placed with the other fabrics. My best advice is to choose fabrics you love. Look at other quilts and color combinations for inspiration, and have fun.

The following should be considered for fabric grain lines in machine appliqué. For methods that use a seam allowance – the invisible appliqué and template and starch methods – it is easier to turn the seam allowances when the curve of the appliqué piece is placed on the bias of the fabric. An example would be to place the curved side of leaves along the bias of the fabric (Fig. 1–4). Most appliqué pieces, such as flowers, have many curved edges and the curves will end up on both the straight and the bias of the fabric (Fig. 1–5). It is helpful to

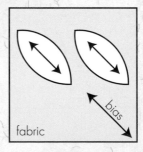

Fig. 1–4. The curved edge of patterns are placed on the bias of fabric.

bias

fabric

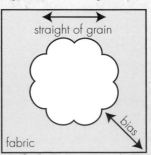

Fig. 1–5. Curves of flower petals are on both the straight and the bias grain of fabric.

straight of grain

bias

fabric

become proficient at turning the seam allowances on the straight as well as the bias of the fabric.

Ultimately, the most important consideration is how the fabric will look when the appliqué piece is cut out. When using a directional fabric, such as a plaid or stripe, the appliqué piece should look nice when cut out. Another consideration is the best use of the fabric. Place appliqué pieces on the fabric to use yardage wisely.

When hand appliquéing, many quilters have been told that the grain line on the appliqué pieces should match the grain line on the background. If the quilter cuts away the background behind the appliqué, it produces a more stable block if the grain lines match. I do not do this for my machine-appliquéd quilts. The main reason is my blocks have so many small pieces that it would be mind boggling to think this through, and the blocks do not seem to lack stability. The only time I try to match the grain line is on

a larger piece, like a basket. It looks better if the grain line of the basket matches the grain line of the background (Fig. 1–6).

Finally, use the best quality of fabric you can. A lot of time will be spent making a beautiful quilt, so why not use the very best fabric.

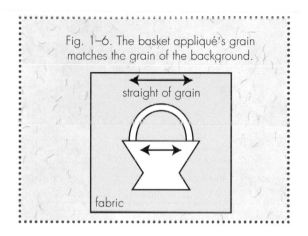

Fig. 1–6. The basket appliqué's grain matches the grain of the background.

straight of grain

fabric

Close-up of FOLK GARDEN ROSE TREE.

Section Two:

Techniques

INVISIBLE APPLIQUÉ

The invisible appliqué method is the most popular technique of the three described in this book. It is easy to do and provides a great finished result. This technique looks the most like hand appliqué. In fact, this technique was called "hand appliqué by machine" in my early classes. When first researching machine appliqué, my focus was to find a method that looked like hand appliqué.

This technique uses a freezer paper pattern and a seam allowance that is turned and secured to the paper with a glue stick. The preparation of the appliqué piece is the most time-consuming part of this method. The result, however, is a precise and accurately prepared appliqué piece. The stitching is done using a blind hem stitch with nylon thread. This makes the stitches appear hand appliquéd and because the stitching is invisible rather than decorative, it goes very fast. It is suitable for many different appliqué projects.

This method works the best with simple to intermediate appliqué designs. Designs with small, intricate pieces may be more suited to the raw-edge fusible method, which is discussed later in this book.

The last step in the invisible appliqué method is cutting away the background to remove the freezer paper. This should not present a problem since the quilt block remains secure, just as a pieced block with seam allowances. For most quilters, the positive aspects of this technique far outweigh what might be this one negative aspect of having to remove the freezer paper. Accurate preparation, easy stitching, and a wonderful invisible finished result make this method one of my favorites.

Preparing Appliqué Pieces

SUPPLY CHECKLIST
(see Supplies, page 18, for detailed description)

- Fabric
- Freezer paper
- Glue stick
- Iron
- Pencil
- Scissors (paper and fabric)
- Spray bottle
- Tweezers
- Washcloth

TRACING APPLIQUÉ PATTERNS

Choose a pattern. Make a full-size drawing of the pattern, following instructions in the pattern section. A photocopy can be used instead of a drawing if desired. Use the drawing or photocopy to trace individual appliqué pieces. These drawings can also be used as a guide for positioning appliqué pieces on the background block.

Trace the appliqué designs individually on the dull side of the freezer paper. The shiny side is melted to temporarily adhere to the fabric. It does not leave residue or harm fabric in any way. Use a sharp pencil to trace the pattern. Do not use pens as ink might transfer onto the fabric.

If the pattern is asymmetrical, trace the design from the reverse side. An example of this is the Wind-Blown Tulip pattern which is blowing to the left. If it is not traced from the reverse, the final appliquéd tulip would be bending to the right.

A freezer paper pattern is needed for each piece in the block because the patterns are not reusable. Cut out each pattern with paper scissors exactly on the traced line (Fig. 2–1 on the following page). The

allowance does not need to be included. The result depends on how accurately the freezer paper patterns were traced and cut.

Fig. 2–1. Trace patterns on freezer paper. Do not overlap patterns.

freezer paper

USING FREEZER PAPER

Place the freezer paper pattern shiny side down on the wrong side of the fabric. Leave at least ½" between the freezer paper patterns to allow for fabric seam allowances. See the fabric discussion in the Supplies section, page 20, for information on placing the pattern on fabric and the grain-line relationship.

Using a hot, dry iron, press the pattern pieces to the fabric for about 10 seconds. Use the cotton setting on the iron; although with some irons, this is too hot and may need to be turned down slightly. Carefully move the iron over the paper so the heat will not scorch the freezer paper. The freezer paper should be firmly attached to the fabric. Do not lift the fabric off the ironing board until it cools because bending the fabric could cause the freezer paper to detach slightly. Layering fabric to continue ironing while the previous pieces are cooling will save time (Fig. 2–2).

Fig. 2–2. Press freezer paper patterns to the wrong side of the fabric.

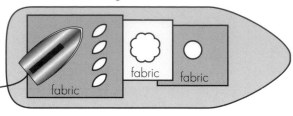

CUTTING FABRIC PIECES

With fabric scissors, cut out appliqué pieces with a ³⁄₁₆" seam allowance. Most quilters use a ¼" seam allowance for piecing, but this is too bulky to turn under. A slightly narrower seam allowance turns much more easily (Fig. 2–3). It is easy to get used to a ³⁄₁₆" seam allowance by cutting around the paper pattern slightly smaller than the usual ¼". Lay the cut edge along the lines in Fig. 2–3 to check the seam allowance. It is also important not to cut the seam allowance too small because it would be difficult to turn. Every pattern piece needs the ³⁄₁₆" seam allowance cut out around all sides.

Fig. 2–3. Allowance guides.

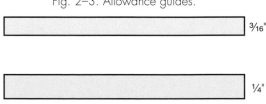

Pattern pieces with inside points and curves will need clipping. For inside points, clip to just shy of the freezer paper, within one or two threads. For inside curves, clip along the inside of the curve halfway to the freezer paper, enough to release the fabric when turning the seam allowance (Fig. 2–4 on the following page). Outside points and curves do not need clipping.

Fig. 2–4. Clip inside points just short of freezer paper.

inside point

freezer paper pattern

Clip inside curves halfway to paper.

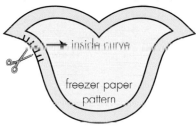

inside curve

freezer paper pattern

TURNING SEAM ALLOWANCES

With a fabric glue stick, turn the ³⁄₁₆" fabric seam allowance to the freezer paper side of the appliqué piece. Start by carefully placing a small amount of glue on the seam allowance on the wrong side of the fabric about 1" to 2" at a time. Using your thumbnail or finger, fold the seam allowance to the freezer paper, keeping the folded edge flat and smooth. When gluing circles or partial circles, there may be some ruffling or folds toward the inner edge of the fabric. This is fine as long as the side-turned edge is smooth. At inside points, glue firmly so the raw edges will not show on the right side. Using a wet washcloth, wipe hands frequently to clean off the glue. Continue gluing around the entire piece (Fig. 2–5).

Outside points need special attention when gluing. For average points, such as

leaves, begin gluing along the right edge and continue gluing to the point and off the edge. Continue around the point and down the left side, making sure the fabric is not visible from the front of the leaf. The left side may need to be eased slightly while gluing (Fig. 2–6).

Fig. 2–5. Glue and turn allowance.

freezer paper pattern

freezer paper pattern

inside point

Glue firmly at inside points so threads won't show on the right side.

Fig. 2–6. Glue and turn allowances on points.

allowance
freezer paper pattern
turned allowance

a. Glue and turn right allowance.

freezer paper pattern
turned allowance

b. Glue and turn left allowance.

OVERLAPPING PIECES

For overlapping pieces, do not glue the edges that lie underneath others. Double slash lines on patterns indicate where an appliqué piece lies underneath another. Mark the pieces that lie underneath others with double slash lines on the freezer paper pattern as a reminder not to glue these edges under. Analyze every appliqué pattern in advance to determine how it will layer and where this marking will need to be done.

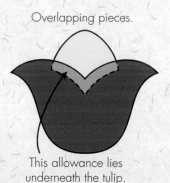

Overlapping pieces.

This allowance lies underneath the tulip.

Glue and turn these two allowances.

Do not glue and turn this allowance.

For really sharp points, such as a tulip tip, an additional step is needed. Starting from the right side, glue off the point as indicated previously. Continue around the left side; however, the point will be too sharp to ease the fabric so it cannot be seen from the front. The result is a little tab that can be seen from the front. Glue that tab and fold it back into the point to hide it, making a tri-fold (Fig. 2–7). This makes a nice sharp point. It is a little thick, but will not be noticed when the quilt is finished. Do not clip any fabric off at the point because it will fray when the stitching is done. Repeat the gluing process for all appliqué pieces in your block.

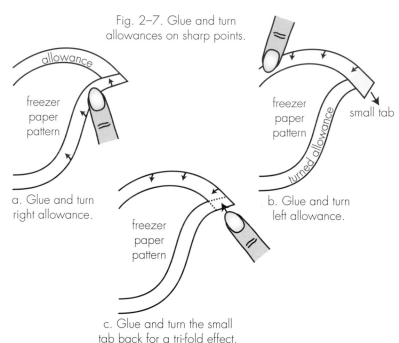

Fig. 2–7. Glue and turn allowances on sharp points.

allowance

freezer paper pattern

a. Glue and turn right allowance.

freezer paper pattern

small tab

turned allowance

b. Glue and turn left allowance.

freezer paper pattern

c. Glue and turn the small tab back for a tri-fold effect.

PLACING APPLIQUÉ PIECES

Cut the background fabric at least 1" larger than the finished size of the block. For example, for a 10" block, cut the background square 11". When machine stitching, the edges of the block can fray and distort, and it is helpful to start with a larger background block. After the machine appliqué is done, rotary cut the appliqué blocks to the correct size, including seam allowances. This method creates a fresh, clean edge for sewing the block together.

For this method, stabilizer is rarely used on the background fabric. The only exception is if the background fabric is a loosely woven or soft fabric. Use spray starch to stiffen this type of fabric before machine appliquéing.

Center the background block over the full-size pattern. If the fabric is dark, use a light box under the pattern. Position the appliqué pieces accurately on the background by using the full-size pattern as a guide. Have multiple-layered units stitched and ready to sew, following the instructions on the right.

Using straight pins, pin all appliqué pieces to the background. At this point, the pieces are ready to stitch.

Stitching Appliqué Pieces

The blind hem stitch is perfect for the invisible method. The stitch can be shortened in width and length to give the appearance of a hand appliqué stitch. By using transparent nylon thread on the top, the stitching is invisible and gives a wonderful look to the project. The freezer paper acts as a stabilizer while the edge of the appliqué piece is being stitched, and it helps to create a clean edge. Because the stitches are small and close together, a 60-weight embroidery thread should be used in the bobbin to keep excess thread from building up and becoming noticeable on the background. The stitching goes surprisingly fast because it is an invisible look, not a decorative one. The result of using the blind hem stitch and invisible thread is a beautiful finished block, giving the appearance of hand work with the ease of machine appliqué.

SUPPLY CHECKLIST
(see Supplies, page 18, for detailed description)

- 60-weight 100% cotton embroidery thread
  (color to match background)
- 70/10 universal needle
- Open-toe appliqué foot
- Sewing machine
- Transparent nylon thread

BLIND HEM STITCH

Most machines have a blind hem stitch that does three to four straight stitches in the background and a zigzag stitch into the appliqué (Fig. 2–8). The goal is to shorten the stitch length and width so the stitching has the appearance of hand appliqué.

The settings for individual machines vary. Set your machine so

Fig. 2–8. Blind hem stitch.

appliqué | background

STITCHING MULTIPLE-LAYERED UNITS BEFORE PINNING

When preparing appliqué pieces that have multiple layers, such as a flower that has a large flower, smaller inner flower, and a center circle, some stitching should be done before it is pinned to the background. Using straight pins, pin the center circle to the small flower and stitch with a blind hem stitch. Next, pin this unit to the large flower and stitch it with the blind hem stitch. The flower unit is now ready to pin to the background with the other appliqué pattern pieces.

Multiple-layered units

a. Stitch center circle to small flower.

b. Stitch small flower unit to larger flower.

the stitch is about ⅟₁₆" wide and ⅟₁₆" long. It is a very small stitch length, similar to a hand appliqué stitch. The width should be about as deep as the hand appliqué stitch would bite into the appliqué piece to hold it down. The bite, or width, needs to be deep enough to catch the fabric. If it is too short, it will not secure the appliqué piece and the edge may fray. Some sewing machines have a slightly different stitch and may need to be adjusted accordingly. Some machines have a blind hem stitch that does a little zigzag on the background and a big zigzag into the appliqué. This can work if adjusted properly, but it will have a slightly different look.

Practice stitching to test the machine's settings. Fold a small piece of fabric so it appears that the fold is being appliquéd to the background. Use an open-toed appliqué foot to have a clear view of the stitching. A size 70/10 universal needle should be used with nylon thread. Thread the sewing machine with transparent nylon thread on the top. See Supplies, page 19, for instructions on nylon thread. Use 60-weight 100% cotton embroidery thread in the bobbin in a color to match the background. Remember that the background will change throughout a project depending on what piece is being sewn, so change the bobbin thread to match.

It is important to keep the straight stitches on the background as close to the appliqué piece as possible (Fig. 2–9). If the straight stitch is not close, it can look sloppy. If your machine has a variable needle position, use the farthest right setting and the inside edge of the right toe on the open-toed appliqué foot to guide you close to the edge of the piece. With

some machines, the needle position moves automatically for this stitch.

Fig. 2–9a. Anatomy of the blind hem stitch.

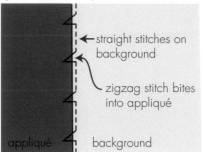

b. Correct: Stitch close to appliqué piece with right toe of foot next to the edge.

c. Incorrect: Straight stitches are too far away from the appliqué piece.

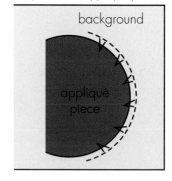

CHECKING TENSION

Once the best stitch width and length have been determined, check the tensions. If the bobbin thread is showing on the top of the piece, loosen the top tension setting slightly. In other words, if the

setting is 4, move it to 3. Sometimes, loosening the top tension is not enough and the bobbin tension may need to be tightened. To tighten the bobbin tension, small adjustments are needed. Locate the tiny screw on your bobbin case. Move the screw clockwise in "five-minute" increments. To tighten the bobbin tension, turn the screw slightly to the right (Fig. 2–10). Also, remember the original position on the bobbin screw so it can be returned to that position when done. Some sewing machine dealers do not recommend adjusting the bobbin tension.

Fig. 2–10. Tighten the bobbin tension. Turn the screw slightly to the right.

STITCHING APPLIQUÉ PIECES

With the stitch settings perfected, the appliqué pieces can be stitched to the background fabric. The freezer paper is still on all the appliqué pieces. It should not be removed from any piece until all stitching is complete.

Stitch the multiple-layered units first. Next, with all appliqué pieces pinned to the background, determine the order of stitching. Stitch continuously around all appliqué pieces on the block (Fig. 2–11). When sewing continuously, there will be times when you will have to stitch to a certain point and then lift the needle out of the fabric, pull the thread across the fabric, and continue stitching to complete the block (Fig. 2–12). Once stitching is complete on the block, clip the threads that were pulled across the fabric. To secure the stitching at the beginning and the end, sew into the beginning

stitches about ⅛". The stitches are so small that both sides will be locked. Clip threads close to the fabric on the front and back (Fig. 2–13).

Fig. 2–11. Stitch continuously around all appliqué pieces following the arrows.

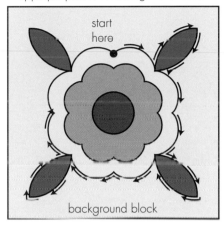

Fig. 2–12. Stitch overlapping pieces.

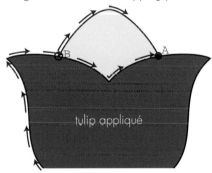

Stitch following arrows, stopping at Point A. Pull threads across tulip tip back to Point B and continue following the arrows.

Fig. 2–13. Overlap the stitching to secure the ends. Clip threads close to the fabric.

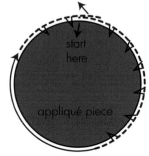

PIVOTING

It is important to pivot while stitching around the curved appliqué pieces. If this is not done often, the background can be distorted. Pivot with the needle in the right-hand swing or in the background.

Pivot with needle in the right swing of the stitch (or background).

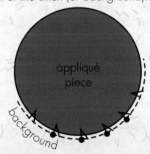

Removing Freezer Paper

One of the last steps for this method is to remove the freezer paper from the appliqué pieces. Cut away the background behind the appliqué pieces, leaving a generous ¼" seam allowance (Fig. 2–14). For stems, cut a slit in the background to allow access to the paper. Be careful not to cut through to the front of the appliqué piece.

Fig. 2–14. Cut out background fabric ¼" away from stitching, then remove freezer paper.

Using warm water, spray the back of the block. Make sure to wet the freezer paper and the seam allowance. It is important to wet the glue in the seam allowance to help release the freezer paper. Let the water soak the paper and glue for about five minutes. (Fabric may run or bleed if it has not been pre-washed and tested. See the fabric discussion in the Supplies section, page 20.)

Gently pull the freezer paper away from the appliqué piece. The stitching will have serrated the edge of the paper, which helps in removing the paper from the fabric and stitching. Occasionally, the freezer paper may be difficult to remove in a sharp point. A pair of tweezers can be helpful to pull the paper out. For multiple-layered units, once the first layer of freezer paper has been removed, cut away the next layer of fabric to get to the next freezer paper layer. Wet the paper and repeat until all layers have been removed. After all the freezer paper has been removed, let the block air dry flat. When dry, the block can be pressed.

Pressing the Blocks

When pressing a block that has nylon thread, do not use a hot iron directly on the nylon. Always turn the iron down to a medium setting and use a pressing cloth between the iron and the block. The nylon thread is heat sensitive and might melt. Also, do not iron the block when it is wet. This might cause the appliqué fabrics to bleed onto the background fabric.

Close-up of ALBERTA ROSE by the author.

Close-up of the border in LET IT GROW by the author.

TEMPLATE AND STARCH APPLIQUÉ

The template and starch method is another popular choice for machine appliqué. It is ideal for the classic appliqué blocks that have traditional shapes and repeat motifs. In this method, a template of the pattern piece is made from heat-resistant template plastic and is used as a guide on the fabric. An advantage to this method is the template is reusable. For a block that contains many of the same pattern pieces, this is a real bonus.

This technique uses a seam allowance that is moistened with liquid starch, turned around the template, and ironed in place. The result is a beautifully prepared appliqué piece. Many hand appliquérs use the technique to this point and then hand appliqué the piece to the background. For machine appliqué, the piece is machine stitched to the background with a blanket stitch. Black or dark thread can be used to give the appearance of the 1930s antique quilts with a hand appliqué blanket stitch. See the Blanket Stitched Butterfly Quilt on page 12 for an example.

In researching this method, I found it had a basis in traditional antique quilts and could be done on the machine. I was ready to have my machine stitching create a decorative look. Machine stitching can give traditional blocks a wonderful blanket-stitched look, which is similar to the hand blanket stitch.

The template and starch method can also be used with a straight-stitched application for a nice result. The straight stitch works well on stems and vines where the blanket stitch might be too bulky. Straight-stitch stems were done frequently by quilters when the sewing machine was first available.

The success of this technique comes from the precisely prepared appliqué piece and the beautiful machine stitching on the edge, creating a lovely traditional block.

Preparing Appliqué Pieces

SUPPLY CHECKLIST
(see Supplies, page 18, for detailed description)

- Cotton swab or small paint brush
- Fabric
- Heat-resistant template plastic
- Iron
- Nail file
- Pencil
- Scissors (paper and fabric)
- Small appliqué straight pins
- Spray starch

MAKING TEMPLATES

Follow the directions in the invisible appliqué method for "Tracing appliqué patterns," page 23.

Trace appliqué designs individually on heat-resistant template plastic with a sharp pencil. One template is all that is needed for repeat pattern pieces because the template is reusable. Trace the exact pattern (Fig. 2–15). A seam allowance does not need to be added to the template.

Fig. 2–15. Trace the templates.

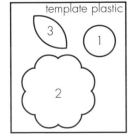

Carefully cut out each template with paper scissors. Because the templates are reusable, take care to make the best template possible. It should have smooth curves and be very accurate. A nail file can be used to sand the edges so the template is smooth (Fig. 2–16).

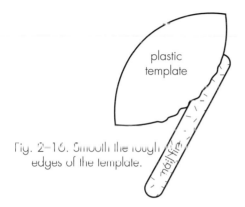

Fig. 2–16. Smooth the rough edges of the template.

Indicate the right side on each template as well as how many appliqué pieces are needed for the block (Fig. 2 17). Place the template right side down on the wrong side of the fabric. Using a fabric marking pencil, carefully trace around the template (Fig. 2–18). Leave about ½" between appliqué pieces to allow for turn-under allowances. Continue until all appliqué pieces have been traced for the block.

Fig. 2–17. Label and number plastic templates.

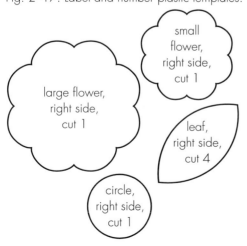

Fig. 2–18. Trace around the template with a marking pencil.

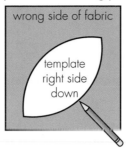

CUTTING FABRIC PIECES

Follow the directions in the invisible appliqué method for Cutting fabric pieces, page 24.

Pattern pieces with inside points and curves will need clipping. For inside points, clip to just before the marked line to release the allowance. For inside curves, clip along the inside of the curve halfway to the marked line, enough to release the curve when turning the allowance (Fig. 2–19 on the following page). Outside points and curves do not need clipping.

Place the template on the fabric appliqué piece with the fabric wrong side up and the template right side down.

TURNING ALLOWANCES

Pour a small amount of liquid spray starch in a cup. Using a cotton swab or small paintbrush, wet the allowance of the appliqué piece, about 1" to 2" at a time. With the front edge (not the tip) of a dry, hot iron, turn the allowance over onto the template. The iron will dry the starch and the allowance will stay crisply turned. Make sure the edge of the appliqué piece is smooth. If folds or

bumps appear, rewet the allowance with starch and try again for a better result. It is okay to have some ruffles or folds in the interior area of the allowance, just not along the edge (Fig. 2–20).

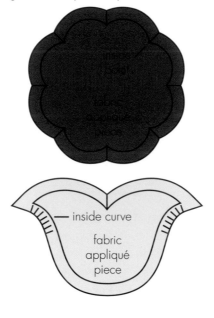

Fig. 2–19. Clip inside points and curves.

inside curve

fabric appliqué piece

Fig. 2–20. Starch and turn allowance over template plastic.

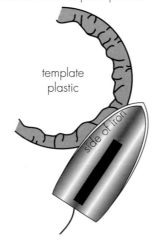

template plastic

side of iron

Continue ironing around the appliqué piece until all of the allowance has been turned. Do not heat the entire template with the iron. Stay on the edge of the template only. Template plastic is only heat resistant

to a certain point. If the whole template is heated, it can become distorted.

It is helpful to have a hard, flat ironing surface. If the ironing board is soft, the appliqué piece and template may sink into the soft surface, making the edge hard to turn. Refer to the ironing board discussion in the Supplies section, page 18. When the allowances have been turned, remove the template. The allowance may need to be released by sliding your fingernail between the template plastic and the fabric. Press the entire appliqué piece once the template plastic has been removed. Do not wet the piece again because the carefully pressed allowance will open.

Points need special attention when starching the allowance. Refer to the invisible appliqué method for Turning seam allowances, second paragraph, page 25. In the template and starch method, however, the seam allowances should be starched and pressed instead of glued.

Mark overlapping pieces with double slash lines on the template as a reminder not to turn this edge under. Refer to Overlapping pieces, page 26.

PLACING APPLIQUÉ PIECES

Follow the directions in the invisible appliqué method for Placing appliqué pieces, page 26.

Center the background block over the full-size pattern. If the fabric is dark, use a light box under the pattern.

Refer to page 27, Multiple-layered Units, of the invisible appliqué method for prepar-

ing these appliqué pieces. Use the blanket stitch instead of the blind hem stitch for the template and starch method.

Using small appliqué straight pins, pin all appliqué pieces to the background. Using the small appliqué pins is helpful because the appliqué pieces should be pressed before stitching. This helps the appliqué pieces lie flat. Large pins with round heads are difficult to press.

Stitching Appliqué Pieces

The blanket stitch is the perfect choice for the template and starch method. It gives a beautiful look on the edge of the appliqué. Use an average to large blanket stitch for this method. The appliqué piece has a turned edge so the stitch needs to hold only the appliqué in place. It does not need to cover a raw edge as a small, close stitch would. With this method, you have the option of using a larger decorative blanket stitch, similar to the 1930 Sunbonnet Sue quilts. Black or dark thread may be used for stitching to give the look of the traditional blanket stitch on antique quilts. Other color threads may also be used.

The blanket stitch is decorative, so care should be taken when stitching, for good results. A straight stitch can also be used with this method if you do not have a blanket stitch on your machine. The straight stitch can be used on stems and vines for a different look along with the blanket stitch on the other appliqué pieces. If the stem is narrow, the blanket stitch can look bulky, while the straight stitch looks neater. Use a matching color cotton thread when straight stitching.

Nylon thread can be used for an invisible option.

SUPPLY CHECKLIST
(see Supplies, page 18, for detailed description)

- 50-weight 100% cotton thread (black or dark color)
- 80/12 universal needle
- Open-toed appliqué foot
- Self-threading needle
- Sewing machine
- Stiletto or large straight pin

BLANKET STITCH
The hand blanket stitch is shown in Fig. 2–21 for comparison. The settings for individual machines vary. Set your machine so the stitch is ⅛" wide and ⅛" long. It's recommended that the length and the width be the same number, but I often vary from this. Have some scrap fabric beside the sewing machine to practice the stitch and discover the settings you prefer.

Fold a small piece of scrap fabric so it appears the fold is being appliquéd to the background. Use an open-toed appliqué foot to have a clear view of the stitching. Thread the machine with black

Fig. 2–21. Hand blanket stitch.

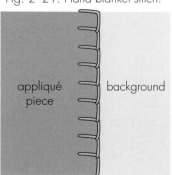

thread or the thread of your choice. Use the same thread color in the bobbin to ensure that the bobbin threads will not show on top.

The blanket stitch includes one stitch on the background, one stitch to the left into the appliqué piece, one stitch back toward the background, one stitch down on the background, and so on (Fig. 2–22).

Fig. 2–22. Anatomy of the blanket stitch.

It is important to keep the straight stitch on the background as close to the appliqué piece as possible (Fig. 2–23a). If the straight stitch is not next to the appliqué piece, it can look sloppy (Fig. 2–23b). If your machine has a variable needle position, move the needle to the farthest right setting and use the inside edge of the right toe on the open-toed appliqué foot to guide your stitching close to the edge of the piece.

On some sewing machines, the blanket stitch is made in the mirror image of the previous description. Instead of starting on the right and stitching to the left, the machine starts on the left and stitches to the right. If the machine has a mirror-image option, use this and the stitch will reverse. If not, the stitch will have to be done from the opposite direction (Fig. 2–24).

Fig. 2–23a. Correct: Stitch is close to appliqué with right toe of foot next to the edge.

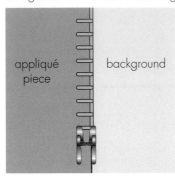

b. Incorrect: Background shows between appliqué and straight stitch.

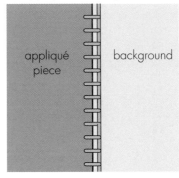

Fig. 2–24. Some machines stitch from left to right.

CHECKING TENSION

Follow the directions in the invisible appliqué method for Checking tension, page 28.

PIVOTING ON CURVES

It is important to keep the left "zig" stitch perpendicular with the straight stitch (Fig. 2–25). Pivot often on curves. Pivot on the right swing or in the background. This keeps the blanket stitch from forming a "V" (Fig. 2–26). On some pieces, it is necessary to pivot every second or third stitch. With small circles, pivot every stitch. Pivot with the needle in the down position. If your machine has a needle-down setting, always use it for the blanket stitch. It is important to learn the stitch and be aware of your position in the stitch at all times. Always stop at the same place in the stitch cycle.

Fig. 2–25. Correct pivoting on curves.

Fig. 2–26. Incorrect pivoting.

STITCHING POINTS

Perfecting the blanket stitch on outside and inside points requires practice.

Outside Points: A leaf has a good outside point for practice (Fig. 2–27). Stitch along the right edge of the leaf until close to the point. Stop with the needle in the background. Remember to be aware of your position in the stitch. Pivot at the point. While perpendicular to the point, do a left "zig" stitch into the point, then a right "zag" stitch back. Pivot and continue down the left edge of the leaf. This takes practice, so do some samples before trying it on the block. It is important to have the point stitched down.

Fig. 2–27. Stitching outside points.

Inside Points: Flowers have good inside points for practice (Fig. 2–28). Stitch along the edge of the flower until close to the inside point. Remember to be aware of your position in the stitch. Pivot at the inside point so the left stitch goes straight into the inside point, then a right zigzag back. Pivot and continue stitching.

Fig. 2–28. Stitching inside points.

Occasionally, the stitch length for the inside or outside point will need to be adjusted slightly so the stitch at the pivot is accurate. This can be done either by backing up a little, lifting the presser foot and backing up slightly to shorten the stitch, or holding back a little with the stitch to shorten it.

STARTING AND STOPPING STITCHES

Begin stitching the appliqué piece away from a point. Otherwise, you will be dealing with two issues at one time: the point and the thread ends. When far enough away from the beginning, stop stitching and pull the starting top thread to the back side of the block (Fig. 2–29). As you begin stitching, hold the bobbin thread away from you so it will not get tangled or sewn onto the back of your work.

Fig. 2–29. Dealing with threads.

a. Pull the starting top thread to the back side when far enough away from the beginning.

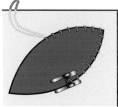

b. When stitching is complete, pull the end top thread to the back side.

c. Tie the four threads in a double knot; clip the threads or use other options.

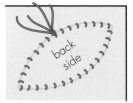

End the stitching at the exact spot you started. The last stitch may have to be adjusted by backing up a little or holding back slightly to shorten the last stitch. Clip the threads, leaving a 6" tail, and pull the end top thread to the back. Tie the two top threads and two bobbin threads in a double knot.

Some other options for handling the thread tails: If the threads do not contrast with the background fabric, simply clip the threads short. If the threads do contrast and would shadow from the front when clipped, choose one of the following options:

- Clip the threads and with a light touch, glue the threads to the darker or non-contrasting fabric.

- Use a self-threading needle (see Supplies, page 19, Fig. 1–2) and thread all four strands by popping them into the needle eye. This saves time because you don't have to thread through the eye of a regular needle. Next, bury the threads between the layers of appliqué and background (Fig. 2–30). Sometimes it is difficult to bring the top thread to the back of the appliqué. If this happens, thread the top thread into the self-threading needle and bring it to the back. The back of the block should look as neat as the front.

Fig. 2–30. Bury threads between the background and appliqué piece.

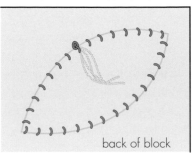

back of block

STITCHING APPLIQUÉ PIECES

When stitching, the appliqué pieces may curl slightly. It is important to press the block before stitching to help the pieces lie flat. Use a stiletto or large straight pin to hold the appliqué in place while stitching.

Begin with multiple-layered units as described in the invisible appliqué method, page 27. After all the pieces have been pinned to the background, begin stitching the appliqué pieces that lie underneath others. Starting the stitch underneath the appliqué piece will help hide the starting and stopping threads. Continue stitching to finish all the appliqué pieces on the block (Fig. 2–31).

Fig. 2–31. Stitch all green leaves, then change thread and stitch the flowers.

STRAIGHT STITCH

With a straight stitch, use 100% cotton thread to match the appliqué fabric. Use the same color of thread in the bobbin. Another option is to use transparent nylon thread to achieve an invisible look. The thread in the bobbin should match the fabric of the appliqué piece.

The straight stitch should be done close to the edge of the appliqué. If it is too far from the edge, it will have a lip. If it is too close to the edge, however, the stitching may fray the fabric slightly. About 1⁄16" from the appliqué edge is perfect. If your machine has a variable needle position, move the needle to the right until it is in position to use the inside edge of the right toe on the open-toed appliqué foot as a guide (Fig. 2–32).

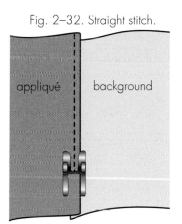

Fig. 2–32. Straight stitch.

appliqué   background

Shorten the stitch length slightly for straight stitch machine appliqué to about 14 to 16 stitches per inch. While stitching around curves, it is difficult to keep a smooth look with a longer stitch length. The longer stitch has a broken look when stitching curves. By shortening the stitch length, the curves will be smoother (Fig. 2–33 on the following page).

Practice the straight stitch until the stitch length and needle position are perfected. Fold a small piece of scrap fabric so it appears that the fold is being appliquéd to the background. Use the open-toed appliqué foot to have a clear view of the stitching. Thread the sewing machine with the thread of your choice. When

Fig. 2–33a. Correct: Curves are smoother with a shorter stitch length.

appliqué piece

b. Incorrect: A longer stitch length looks uneven.

appliqué piece

you're comfortable with your technique and your results, proceed to the next step.

Begin stitching on the block in the same order as described for the blanket stitch. Follow the directions for starting and stopping stitches as described in the blanket stitch, page 38.

You can straight stitch all the appliqué pieces with this method or you can choose to do only the stems and vines. Another option for stems and vines is to use a bias strip of fabric that is turned under ¼" on both sides and basted in place on the background. Straight stitch machine appliqué the stem in place. Refer to bias-strip stems, page 47, in the raw-edge fusible method for a detailed description.

Close-up of WILD ROSES IN THE WOODS by Carol Spaly.

RAW-EDGE FUSIBLE APPLIQUÉ

The raw-edge fusible method is a wonderful choice for machine appliqué. This is an ideal method for more intricate appliqué blocks with small and fussy pieces. The results are accurate and precise with sharp points and neat corners. There are no allowances to turn under, so preparation time is faster than the previous two methods.

In the past, quilters have not liked the finished result when using the raw-edge fusible technique. The fusible web can make the quilt less pliable, particularly when used in multiple layers. With the method presented here, most of the fusible web is cut away, leaving a ¼" outline of the web on the outside edge of the appliqué piece. The result is a softer finished product. Many of the new fusible web products are more lightweight.

Another reason quilters have not liked the raw-edge method is that the satin stitch used on the edge of the appliqué made a stiffer finished product. A small blanket stitch can be used on the edge of the appliqué to cover the raw edge. This allows a lovely, softer finished edge. If your machine does not have a blanket stitch, a zigzag stitch will work nicely.

Also covered in this section is the straight-stitch bias-strip method, which is sometimes used for stems and vines with raw-edge fusible blocks. People often ask if the raw-edge fusible method will hold up over time with frequent washing. If a reliable fusible web is used, the bond is permanent. However, the stitching is what secures the appliqué pieces to the background.

Preparing Appliqué Pieces

SUPPLY CHECKLIST
(see Supplies, page 18, for detailed description)
- Fabric
- Iron
- Pencil
- Scissors
- Spray starch
- Stiletto or large straight pin
- Paper-backed fusible web

TRACING APPLIQUÉ PATTERNS
Follow the directions in the invisible appliqué method for Tracing appliqué patterns, page 23.

Trace designs individually on the paper side of the fusible web. Use a sharp pencil for tracing. A fusible web pattern will be needed for each piece in the block.

If the pattern is asymmetrical, trace the design from the reverse side. An example of this is the Wind-Blown Tulip pattern which is blowing to the left. If it is not traced from the reverse, the final appliquéd tulip would be bending to the right.

CUTTING FUSIBLE WEB
Cut fusible web with paper scissors about ¼" larger than the drawn, or fabric cutting, lines. Next, cut about ¼" from the drawn lines on the inside of the fusible web, making a ring of web. Cut directly through the fusible web to get to the inside (Fig. 2–34 on the following page). Repeat the process for all appliqué pieces in the block. Small pieces, such

OVERLAPPING PIECES

Overlapping appliqué pieces need special consideration. Determine which appliqué pieces lie underneath other appliqué pieces. Trace the design on the paper side of the fusible web. Mark the edge that lies underneath another appliqué piece with double slash lines. Cut the fusible web as previously described, leaving extra on the outside and inside drawn lines. When an appliqué piece lies underneath another piece, cut away the fusible web on that edge only, on the drawn line. This will eliminate a double layer of fusible web.

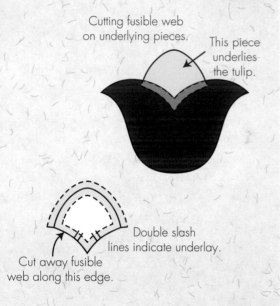

Cutting fusible web on underlying pieces.

This piece underlies the tulip.

Double slash lines indicate underlay.

Cut away fusible web along this edge.

Fuse the prepared piece to the wrong side of the fabric. Cut away on the drawn (cutting) lines *except* for the edge that lies underneath another appliqué piece. On this edge, cut a ¼" allowance of fabric. This allowance will lie under the adjoining appliqué piece.

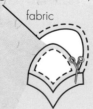

Cutting fabric on underlying pieces.

fabric

Cut on drawn line except for underlay.

as tiny circles and small stems, do not need the fusible web cut away from the inside.

Fig. 2–34. Cut the fusible web along the dashed lines, leaving a ring of web.

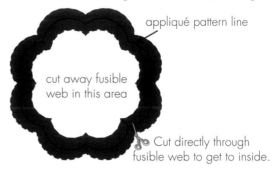

appliqué pattern line

cut away fusible web in this area

Cut directly through fusible web to get to inside.

FUSING APPLIQUÉ PIECES

Place this prepared piece on the wrong side of the fabric. Keep the paper side up and the fusible web down on the wrong side of the fabric. For information on placing the fusible web on fabric and on the grain-line relationship, refer to the fabric discussion in the Supplies section, page 20. Fuse pieces to the fabric with an iron, following the specific instructions for the fusible web being used. The fusible glue does not need to be completely melted at this time, only transferred to the back of the fabric (Fig. 2–35).

Some quilters use a pressing sheet with fusible web. This sheet ensures that the web glue will not adhere to the iron or ironing board in case of an accident. I do not use a pressing sheet; however, I have an iron and ironing surface used only for machine appliqué.

With fabric scissors, cut the appliqué pieces on the drawn line. By taking these steps, there will be a continuous area of fusible web at the edge of the appliqué piece (Fig. 2–36).

Fig. 2–35. Fusing appliqué pieces.

Fig. 2–36. Cut along the drawn line to create a raw-edge appliqué piece.

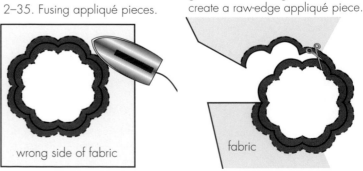

wrong side of fabric

fabric

PLACING APPLIQUÉ PIECES

Follow directions in the invisible appliqué method for Placing appliqué pieces, page 26.

For this raw-edge method, the background square requires a stabilizer. Use spray starch to stiffen the background, following instructions in the Supplies section, page 18, to determine the type to use. Spray starch the background to the stiffness of typing paper. This allows for accuracy when stitching because everything remains flat and even. This method is preferred over using an iron-on stabilizer, such as freezer paper, because it does not have to be torn away.

Center the background block over the full-size pattern. If the fabric is dark, use a light box under the pattern.

Remove the paper backing on the fusible web. Place the appliqué pieces accurately on the background. Use a stiletto or large straight pin to help move small appliqué pieces. Have multiple-layered units stitched and ready to use. If using bias stems, have them ready to baste down. Refer to the straight-stitch bias-strip stem instructions, page 47.

Make sure that overlapping pieces are properly placed. When all pieces have been positioned accurately on the background block, press in place. Gently move the iron over the surface, being careful not to disturb the placement of the appliqué pieces. Once pressed, the pieces cannot be moved. Follow the ironing directions for your specific fusible web.

Stitching Appliqué Pieces

The blanket stitch is my favorite for raw-edge appliqué. It gives a beautiful look on the edge of the appliqué pieces. Because there is not an allowance to turn under, it has a flat look, quite different from the look of methods that use an allowance. A small blanket stitch allows the stitches to stay close together, covering as much of the raw edge as possible. Colorful threads can also be used to enhance this lovely stitch.

If your machine does not have a blanket stitch, a zigzag stitch is another option. I use what I call a flat zigzag to avoid the look of the raised, thick satin stitch. The zigzag

STITCHING MULTIPLE-LAYERED UNITS BEFORE FUSING

When preparing appliqué pieces that have multiple layers, such as a flower that has a large flower, smaller inner flower, and a center circle, stitching is done before fusing it to the background. Fuse the inner flower and center circle to the large flower, leaving paper backing on the bottom flower. Stitch the center circle and inner flower. Remove the paper on the large flower, and fuse it to the background block along with all the other pieces. It is easier to work with these smaller units at the machine before they are fused to the background.

Stitch multiple-layered units before fusing to the background. Leave paper on the back until it is ready to fuse to the completed unit.

gives a different look than the blanket stitch, but works equally well. Straight-stitch bias-strip stems, page 47, may also be used as an option for blocks.

SUPPLY CHECKLIST

(see Supplies, page 18, for detailed description)

- 50-weight 100% cotton thread to match or contrast appliqué (30-weight cotton or any variety of decorative threads may also be used)
- 80/12 universal needles (or appropriate size for decorative thread)
- Open-toed appliqué foot
- Self-threading needle
- Sewing machine

BLANKET STITCH

Follow the directions in the template and starch appliqué method for the Blanket stitch, page 35. For the raw-edge fusible method, set your machine so the stitch is about 1⁄16" wide and 1⁄16" long. It is a small stitch, meant to cover most of the raw edge.

CHECKING TENSION

Follow the directions in the invisible appliqué method for Checking tension, page 28.

PIVOTING ON CURVES

Follow the directions in the template and starch appliqué method for Pivoting on curves, page 37.

STITCHING POINTS

Follow the directions in the template and starch appliqué method for Stitching points, page 37.

STARTING AND STOPPING STITCHES

Follow the directions in the template and starch appliqué method for Starting and stopping stitches, page 38.

STITCHING APPLIQUÉ PIECES

Stitch the multiple-layered units as described on page 43. After all pieces have been fused on the background, begin stitching with one color of thread and complete the stitching of all appliqué pieces that have this color. Next, choose another color of thread and complete all appliqué pieces that have this color, and so on until the block is complete (Fig. 2–37).

Fig. 2–37. Stitch all green leaves, then change thread and stitch flowers.

FLAT ZIGZAG STITCH

If your machine does not have a blanket stitch, the flat zigzag stitch is a wonderful option for raw-edge fusible appliqué. The satin stitch is another popular zigzag stitch choice. However, the stitch length is quite small in the satin stitch. The result is a thick bead of thread along the edge of the appliqué. It is a nice look for clothing, but rather stiff for a quilt. The flat zigzag is a better choice because it has a look and feel similar to the blanket stitch.

The stitch length and width are adjusted on the zigzag stitch to cover the raw edge in a flat, thinner look similar to the blanket stitch. The stitch uses 50-weight, 100% cotton thread that matches or compliments the appliqué piece. Some quilters like the flat zigzag as well as or better than the blanket stitch. It can be used in combination with the blanket stitch for variety in an appliqué block. The flat zigzag is shown in Fig. 2–38.

Fig. 2–38. Flat zigzag stitch.

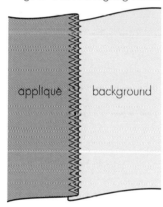

The settings for individual machines vary. Set your machine so the stitch is about ⅛" wide. The setting should be adjusted for the look you prefer.

Practice the stitch on scrap fabric. Fold a small piece of fabric so it appears you are appliquéing the fold to the background. Use an open-toed appliqué foot to have a clear view of the stitching. Thread the sewing machine with the thread of your choice. Use the same color of thread in the bobbin.

The flat zigzag stitch looks like a regular zigzag stitch except it has a shorter stitch length and narrower width. The length should be short enough so it covers the raw edge, but not so small that the thread forms a thick beaded look. It should also be flat. The width should be sufficient to hold the appliqué piece down securely. A stitch width too narrow would fray the raw edge and a stitch width too wide tends to look decorative.

When sewing, the stitch should follow the edge of the appliqué evenly. The left swing of the stitch should go into the appliqué and the right swing of the stitch should be on the background fabric (Fig. 2–39). It is also important to pivot frequently when stitching the inside and outside curves to keep the stitch perpendicular to the appliqué edge. Pivot in the right swing, or background, of the stitch (Fig. 2 40).

Fig. 2–39. Anatomy of the flat zigzag stitch.

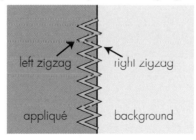

Fig. 2–40. Pivoting. For curves, pivot with the needle down on the background.

If your machine has a variable needle position, set it to the farthest right setting. Use the inside edge of the right toe on the open-toed appliqué foot to guide you close to the edge of the appliqué stitch. Use the needle-down position, if it is available on your machine, when pivoting.

CHECKING TENSION

Follow the directions in the invisible machine appliqué method for Checking tension, page 28.

STITCHING POINTS

Perfecting the zigzag stitch on outside and inside points requires practice.

Outside Points: A leaf has a good outside point for practice. Choose one of the following options to stitch a point with the flat zigzag stitch:

• **Overlapped Point:** Stitch along the right side of the leaf to the edge of the point, stopping at the background fabric. Pivot, adjusting needle and presser foot to line up with the left edge. Continue along the left side of the leaf. The stitching will cover or overlap previous stitching (Fig. 2–41).

Fig. 2–41. Overlapped point.

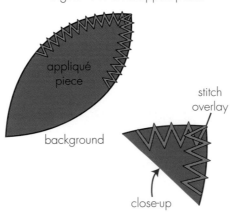

• Tapered point: Stitch along the right side of the leaf, and as you come close to the point, start decreasing the stitch width slowly to zero at the point. Pivot and start stitching down the left side, beginning to increase the stitch width to equal the right side (Fig. 2–42). This takes practice, but it gives a very nice mitered look.

Fig. 2–42. Tapered point.

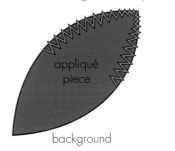

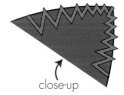

Inside Points: Flowers have good inside points for practice. Stitch along the edge of the flower, right to left, until reaching the inside point. Pivot and make a zigzag stitch into the point. Pivot again and continue around the appliqué piece. Pivot with the needle in the down position and in the right swing or background. It is important to make a stitch in the inside point (Fig. 2–43).

Fig. 2–43. Stitch into the inside point.

STARTING AND STOPPING STITCHES

Follow directions in the template and starch appliqué method for Starting and stopping stitches, page 38, as described for the blanket stitch option.

STITCHING APPLIQUÉ PIECES

Follow the directions in the template and starch machine appliqué method for Stitching appliqué pieces, page 39, Fig. 2–31, as described for the blanket stitch option.

STRAIGHT-STITCH BIAS-STRIP STEM

I often use straight-stitched stems when machine appliquéing. I like to have variety in the stitching on my blocks and am inspired by the straight-stitched stems and vines that adorn many antique quilts. Straight-stitch bias-striping works best with stems that are an even width. A stem that varies in width is better suited to the raw-edge fusible method, which can be used for any of the stems.

CUTTING BIAS STRIPS

Cut a bias strip of fabric. For most of the blocks in the book, a 1" bias strip will work nicely. If the stem is wider, cut the bias strip a little wider. If the stem is more narrow, cut the bias strip a little more narrow. Only a small amount of bias is needed for these blocks. Usually two or three bias strips cut from a fat quarter are sufficient (Fig. 2–44).

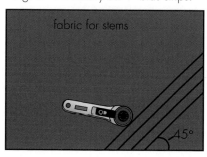

Fig. 2–44. Rotary cut 1" bias strips.

STITCHING BIAS STRIPS

Fold the edges to the center in thirds, overlapping in a tri-fold manner. By hand, baste both edges down (Fig. 2–45). Press firmly to flatten the basted strip. The bias strip is now ready to use.

Fig. 2–45. Baste both edges down by hand.

When straight stitching, use 100% cotton thread to match the fabric. Use the same color of thread in the bobbin. The straight stitch should be done close to the edge of the bias stem. If it is too far from the edge, it will have a lip. If it is too close to the edge, however, the stitching may pull the folded edge slightly; about 1/16" from the appliqué edge is perfect. If your machine has a variable needle position, move the needle to the right until the right toe of the open-toed appliqué foot can be used as a guide.

Shorten the stitch length slightly for straight-stitch machine appliqué. While stitching around curves, it is difficult to keep a smooth look with a longer stitch length. By shortening the stitch length, the curves will appear smoother. See page 40, Fig. 2–33 a and b.

Fold a small piece of scrap fabric so it appears the fold is being appliquéd to the background. Use the open-toed appliqué

foot to have a clear view of the stitching. Thread the sewing machine with the thread of your choice. Practice the straight stitch until the stitch length and needle position are perfected. See page 39, Fig. 2–32.

BIAS-STRIP STEMS ON BLOCKS

To use bias strip stems on blocks, baste the stems on the background before fusing all other appliqué pieces to the background. Lay the background block on the full-size drawing. With a pencil, draw stem placement lines on the background. Cut the bias strips to the proper size. Add about ¼" to the ends of the bias strips that will go under other appliqué pieces. Pin in place and thread baste to the background. Remove the pins. Press firmly to flatten the stems. Fuse the remaining appliqué pieces. The block is now ready for stitching. Remove the basting threads when the stitching is complete.

STARTING AND STOPPING STITCHES

Follow directions in the template and starch appliqué method for Starting and stopping stitches, page 38, as described for the blanket stitch option.

Close-up of LE PANIER DE FLEURS by the author.

APPLIQUÉ VARIATIONS

There are many variations to the techniques in this book. For several reasons, I prefer using the preparations and the stitching options as they have been presented previously. However, you may find the following variations appropriate for a particular project.

Invisible Appliqué

The following variations can be used with the invisible appliqué technique if desired.

FREEZER PAPER OPTIONS

Read Preparing Appliqué Pieces, page 23, to become familiar with the technique. Then try the following variation. Cut out freezer-paper patterns. Iron the freezer-paper patterns to right side of the fabric. Cut out the appliqué pieces with a ³⁄₁₆" allowances. Using a glue stick, glue the allowance to the wrong side of the fabric (Fig. 2–46). When the glue is dry, remove the freezer paper pattern. The appliqué piece is ready for stitching.

Fig. 2–46. Glue and turn the allowance to the wrong side of the appliqué piece.

freezer paper pattern

back of fabric

Freezer paper is on the front.

I find it awkward to do the gluing this way. The advantage is you do not have to cut away the backing to remove the freezer paper from the inside. I do not like the stitching portion as well with this method of preparation. The freezer paper on the inside is a stabilizer and aids in creating a better blind hem stitch.

Additionally, the edge with this method of preparation is more difficult to turn. Folds and bumps on the edge of the appliqué might be difficult to avoid. An option would be to use this method of preparation with a decorative stitch on the edge. A blanket stitch or a straight stitch might work nicely.

You can use this freezer paper method with invisible machine appliqué.

BLANKET STITCH WITH INVISIBLE APPLIQUÉ

If you want to use the blanket stitch for invisible appliqué, keep in mind the following consideration. The success of invisible appliqué comes from how easily the freezer paper can be removed from the blind hem stitching. The stitch is so small that it serrates the freezer paper, making removal easy. If the blanket stitch is used, the freezer paper will be more difficult to remove. The stitch bites deeper, and there are not as many tiny stitches to serrate the paper.

STRAIGHT STITCH WITH INVISIBLE APPLIQUÉ

An invisible straight stitch would not produce a good result because the straight stitch makes the freezer paper difficult to remove. In fact, a small amount of paper invariably remains in the block.

Template & Starch Appliqué

The following variation can be used with the template and starch appliqué technique if desired.

BLIND HEM STITCH

The invisible appliqué method is successful because the freezer paper acts as a stabilizer during sewing with the blind hem stitch. Without the paper stabilizer, the stitch is so small that it can distort the edge of the appliqué piece. The starched edge is only slightly stiff.

Close-up of BLACKBIRDS FLY by the author and Pat Holly.

Close-up of SEPTEMBER ROSE AND BUD by the author.

Section Three:
Quilt Projects
and Patterns

Simple Appliqué Sampler

SIMPLE APPLIQUÉ SAMPLER – 48" x 60".
Machine appliquéd, pieced, and quilted by the author.

MACHINE APPLIQUÉ: A Sampler of Techniques   Sue Nickels

PATTERNS

This sampler quilt is made up of 12 different tulip and rose blocks. The designs are beginner level. They have simple pattern pieces and a minimal number of pieces per block. All three methods are used throughout the quilt, making it a true sampler of techniques. The three methods can be used successfully on each of the 12 blocks. These are great blocks for learning each technique.

The patterns are shown full size. An 8½" finished-size background block is used. When making the blocks, use a flat, full-size pattern. To make the full-size pattern, either trace from the book on a piece of paper with a permanent pen or use a copy machine to copy the pattern onto paper. Tracing paper is great to use for the full-size block drawings. If using a pattern that is asymmetrical, the appliqué patterns need to be traced from the reverse (for the invisible appliqué and raw-edge fusible methods). Turn the tracing paper over and trace the patterns.

Next, using the full-size drawing, trace the appliqué pattern pieces directly onto freezer paper, heat-resistant template plastic, or paper-backed fusible web, depending on the technique used. Follow directions for the technique chosen to complete the block. Indicate on the pattern with double slash lines when an appliqué piece lies underneath another.

Directions for completing this sampler quilt are included. Other options may be used to make your own original quilt. Look in the Gallery, page 103, for inspiration.

SIMPLE APPLIQUÉ SAMPLER PATTERNS

1. Angle-edged Rose
2. Blooming Rose
3. Budding Tulips
4. Cottonball Rose
5. Double Rose
6. Single Rose and Buds
7. Single Tulip
8. Small Rose Wreath
9. Tulip and Bud
10. Tulip and Heart
11. Tulip with Four Leaves
12. Wind-blown Tulip

INSTRUCTIONS

Finished quilt size: 46½" x 58"
Finished block size: 8½" x 8½"

Use 12 appliquéd blocks. Start with an 11" x11" background square and cut down to 9" x 9" after appliquéing the blocks.

YARDAGE

Background blocks	1 yard
Appliqué pieces	(total of 1 yard)
	small amounts of
	a variety of fabric
Nine-patch sashing:	
Light fabric	¾ yard
Dark fabric	1 yard
Outer border	1 yard
Nine patch	scraps
Batting	50½" x 62"
Backing	3 yards
Binding	½ yard
(for 2½" straight-grain binding)	

CONSTRUCTION OF NINE-PATCHES

- Cut five 1½" strips of light fabric across the width of the fabric.
- Cut four 1½" strips of dark fabric across the width of the fabric.

Sew strips together to make one "A" strip set and two "B" strip sets (Fig. 3–1). Press seams toward light fabric.

Fig. 3–1. Sew strips together to make:

A: 1 strip set   **B:** 2 strip sets

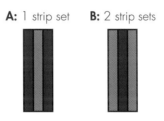

Cut these strip sets into 1½" segments. There should be 20 segments of "A" and 40 segments of "B" (Fig. 3–2).

Fig. 3–2. Sew into 20 nine-patch units (press seams to lighter fabric).

CONSTRUCTION OF SASHING SEGMENTS

- Cut eight 1½" strips of light fabric across the width of the fabric.
- Cut sixteen 1½" strips of dark fabric across the width of the fabric.

Sew together to make eight more "A" strip sets and press toward light fabric. Cut these sets into 9" segments, making a total of 31 segments.

CONSTRUCTION OF QUILT TOP

Place the 12 appliqué blocks in a pleasing arrangement. Sew the quilt top together, press, and measure for the outer border (Figs. 3–3 and 3–4).

Fig. 3–3. Press seam allowances toward appliqué blocks. Sew blocks to sashing segments in rows.

Fig. 3–4. Press seam allowances toward nine-patch units. Sew sashing segments to nine-patch units in rows.

CONSTRUCTION OF OUTER BORDER

Cut five strips 5" wide across the width of the fabric. Use two strips for the top and bottom borders. Cut one strip in half. Add these to the remaining two strips for the side borders. Measure across the center of the quilt. Cut borders the correct width and length. Sew top and bottom borders.

Make four nine-patch units by cutting 2" strips of scraps. Follow the directions given previously for nine-patches. Four 5" unfinished nine-patches will be needed for the corners.

Add borders and nine-patch corners to complete the quilt top. Layer with batting and backing. Baste and quilt as desired. Bind to finish.

Quilt assembly.

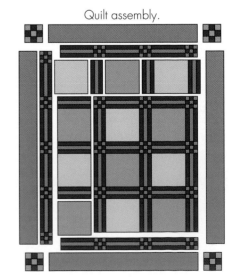

Angle-Edged Rose

Blooming Rose

MACHINE APPLIQUÉ: A Sampler of Techniques

Sue Nickels

Budding Tulips

Double slash lines indicate when an appliqué piece lies underneath another.

Cottonball Rose

Double slash lines
indicate when an appliqué
piece lies underneath another.

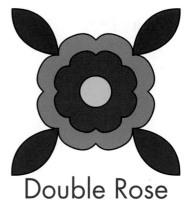

Double Rose

Single Rose
and Buds

Double slash lines
indicate when an appliqué
piece lies underneath another.

MACHINE APPLIQUÉ: A Sampler of Techniques   *Sue Nickels*

Single Tulip

Small Rose Wreath

Double slash lines
indicate when an appliqué
piece lies underneath another.

The raw-edge fusible method works best
on this block because of the small pieces.

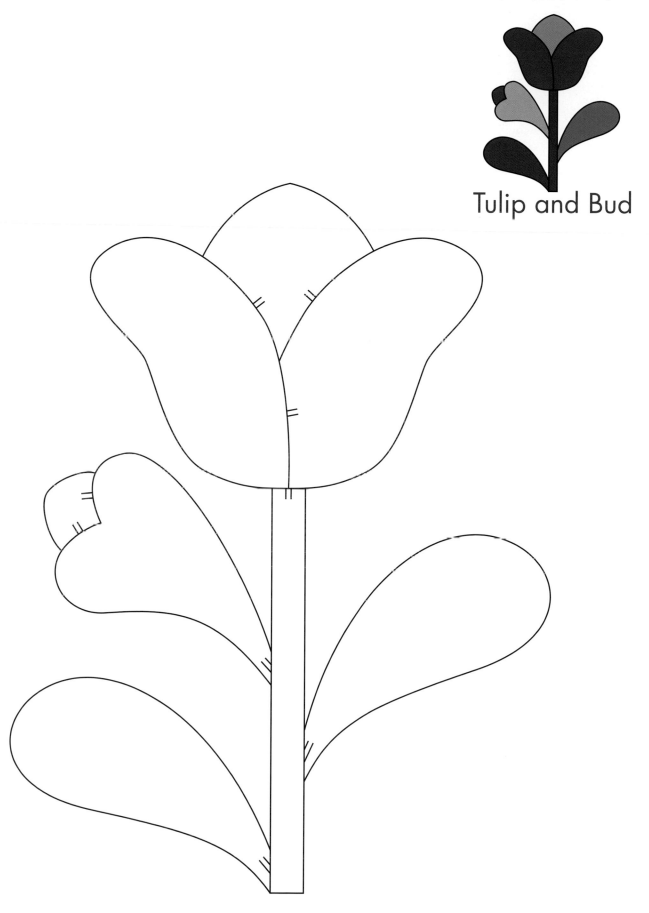

Tulip and Bud

Tulip and Heart

Double slash lines indicate when an appliqué piece lies underneath another.

Double slash lines
indicate when an appliqué
piece lies underneath another.

Tulip with Four Leaves

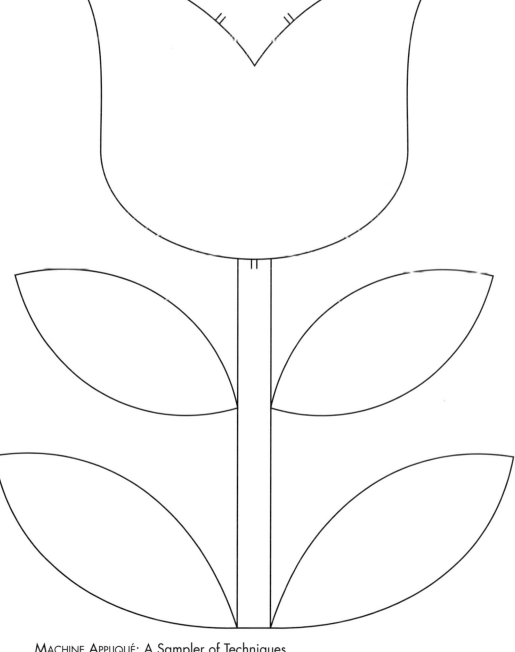

Wind-blown Tulip

Double slash lines
indicate when an appliqué
piece lies underneath another.

Trace this asymmetrical pattern
from the reverse side as explained
in the invisible and raw-edge
fusible appliqué techniques.

CLASSIC APPLIQUÉ SAMPLER – 63" x 80".

Machine appliquéd, pieced, and quilted by the author.

PATTERNS

This sampler quilt is made up of 12 different classic appliqué blocks. The designs are intermediate level. The patterns are more complex with more pieces per block. The template and starch and the raw-edge fusible methods are used on this quilt. It would also be appropriate to use the invisible appliqué method for these blocks.

When designing the blocks for this quilt, my inspiration was the classic appliqué patterns I have admired over the years. I chose my four favorite classic appliqué patterns and designed three blocks for each pattern. The four patterns are the Rose of Sharon, the Rose Wreath, the Whig Rose, and the Rose Tree. I was interested in making intermediate-level quilt blocks with machine techniques by using the traditional patterns that have inspired quilters over the years.

A 15" finished-size background block is used. Most patterns shown are a quarter of the block. The Rose Tree patterns, however, show half of the block. Use a full-size pattern when making the blocks.

To make a full-size pattern, use a 15" square of tracing paper and fold it in quarters. Open the tracing paper and, with a permanent pen, trace one quarter of the block, aligning dashed lines on the pattern with fold lines on the tracing paper. Repeat three more times to complete a full-size drawing (Fig. 3–5). The patterns may be easier to trace if a photocopy is used.

The Rose Tree patterns are shown with a bottom quarter of the pattern on one page and a top quarter of the pattern on a second page. For these blocks, fold a 15" square of tracing paper in quarters. Open the tracing paper and, with a permanent pen, trace the lower-right quarter and the upper-right quarter of the pattern, aligning the broken lines. Fold the tracing paper in half and trace the left half from the right half that is already drawn (Fig. 3–6).

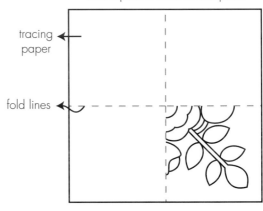

Fig. 3–5. Trace ¼" pattern from book and repeat 3 times to complete.

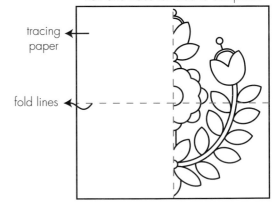

Fig. 3–6. On the Rose Tree patterns, trace upper- and lower-right patterns from book. Fold tracing paper in half and trace left side to complete.

Using the full-size pattern, trace the appliqué pattern pieces directly on the freezer paper, heat-resistant template plastic, or paper-backed fusible web, depending on the technique used. Follow

the directions for the technique chosen to complete your block. If the pattern is asymmetrical, the appliqué patterns need to be traced from the reverse for the invisible appliqué and raw-edge fusible appliqué methods. Indicate on the pattern when one appliqué piece lies under another by using double slash lines. Special considerations are mentioned with each block.

Directions for completing this sampler quilt are included. Other options can be used to make your own original quilt. Look in the Gallery, page 103, for inspiration.

CLASSIC APPLIQUÉ SAMPLER PATTERNS

1. Album Rose Tree
2. Cross-stem Rose Tree
3. Dahlia Wreath
4. Rose of Sharon
5. Fancy Wreath
6. Roses and Buds
7. Roses, Roses, Roses
8. Rose Tree
9. Rose with Tulips
10. Rose Wreath
11. Traditional Whig Rose
12. Whig Rose

INSTRUCTIONS

Finished quilt size: 63" x 80"
Finished block size: 15" x 15"

Use 12 appliquéd blocks. Start with a 17" x 17" background square and cut down to 15½" x 15½" after appliquéing the blocks.

YARDAGE

Background blocks	2¾ yards
Appliqué pieces	variety of fabrics to equal 2½ yards

Sashing	1 yard
Cornerstones	½ yard
Outer border	1½ yards
Corner blocks	¼ yard
Batting	67" x 84"
Backing	4 yards
Binding	¾ yard
	(for 2½" straight-grain binding)

PREPARATION OF SASHING SEGMENTS

• Cut thirty-one 2½" x 15½" strips from the sashing fabric.
• Cut twenty 2½" x 2½" squares from the cornerstone fabric.

CONSTRUCTION OF QUILT TOP

Place the 12 appliqué blocks in a pleasing arrangement. Sew the appliqué blocks to the sashing strips in rows. Press seams toward sashing strips (Fig. 3–7).

Sew the sashing strips to the cornerstone squares in a row. Press seams toward sashing strips (Fig. 3–8).

Sew the appliqué rows to the sashing rows, referring to the assembly diagram of the quilt on page 70.

Fig. 3–7. Sew appliqué blocks to sashing strips.

Fig. 3–8. Sew sashing strips to cornerstone squares.

CONSTRUCTION OF OUTER BORDER

Cut five 5½" strips from the length of the border fabric. Use two strips for the top and bottom borders. Cut one strip in half and add the pieces to the remaining two strips for side borders. Measure across the center of the quilt for accurate size. Cut borders the correct width and length. Sew top and bottom borders.

Cut four 5½" squares from the corner fabric. Add the squares to the ends of the remaining borders. Sew side borders to complete quilt top. Press seams toward borders.

Layer with batting and backing. Baste and quilt as desired. Bind to finish. My quilt has a small red piping between the sashing and outer border for a decorative touch.

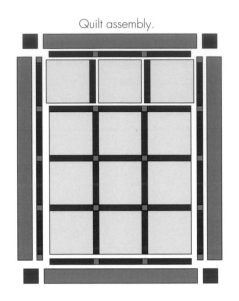

Quilt assembly.

Close-up of CLASSIC APPLIQUÉ SAMPLER Traditional Whig Rose block by the author.

Album Rose Tree

(2-page pattern)

Cut a bias strip 1" x 18",
if using a straight-stitch
bias stem for this block.

Sign and date in large
heart with a permanent pen.

Double slash lines
indicate when an appliqué
piece lies underneath another.

Double slash lines indicate when an appliqué piece lies underneath another.

Album Rose Tree

(2-page pattern)

Use this guide when tracing
the cross in the stem.

Cross-stem Rose Tree

(2-page pattern)

Cross-stem Rose Tree
(2-page pattern)
The straight-stitch bias-strip stem method
is not a good choice for this block.

Sue Nickels

Double slash lines
indicate when an appliqué
piece lies underneath another.

Dahlia Wreath

For the center flower, use the flower
from the Fancy Wreath pattern.

Fancy Wreath

MACHINE APPLIQUÉ: A Sampler of Techniques

Sue Nickels

Double slash lines
indicate when an appliqué
piece lies underneath another.

Rose of Sharon

Rose with Tulips

Broken lines indicate where
stitching or small stems may be used.

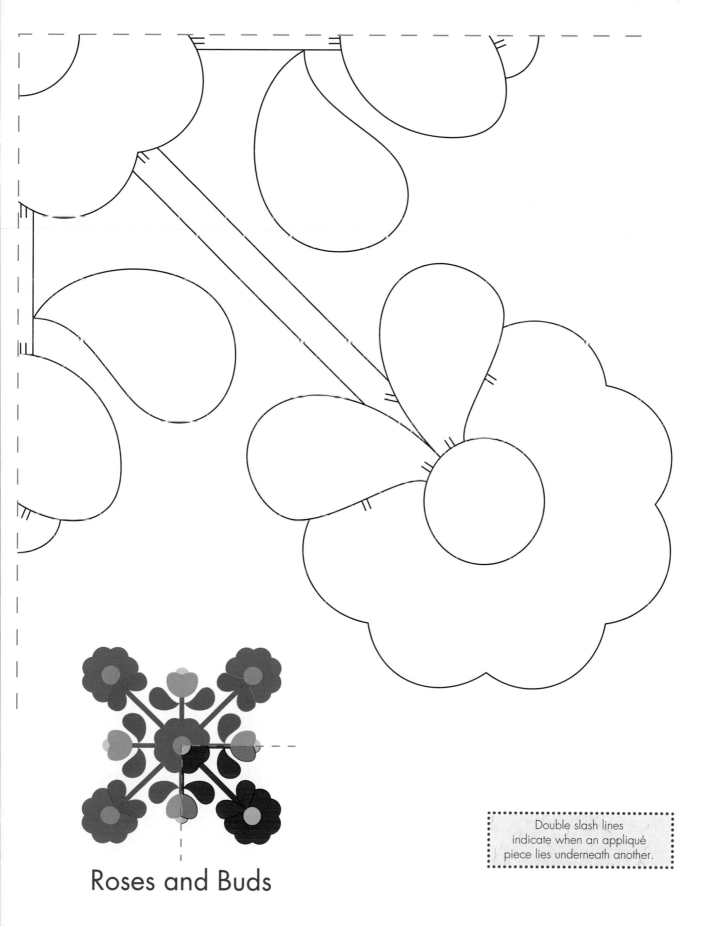

Double slash lines
indicate when an appliqué
piece lies underneath another.

Roses and Buds

Use this center flower unit
when tracing the full-size pattern.

Roses, Roses, Roses

MACHINE APPLIQUÉ: A Sampler of Techniques   *Sue Nickels*

Double slash lines
indicate when an appliqué
piece lies underneath another.

Rose Tree
(2-page pattern)

Cut a bias strip 1" x 18", if using a
straight-stitch bias-strip stem for this block.

Double slash lines indicate when an appliqué piece lies underneath another.

Rose Tree
(2-page pattern)

Broken lines indicate where stitching or small stems may be used.

Rose Wreath

Double slash lines
indicate when an appliqué
piece lies underneath another.

Traditional Whig Rose

MACHINE APPLIQUÉ: A Sampler of Techniques *Sue Nickels*

Whig Rose

Folk Garden Appliqué Sampler

FOLK GARDEN APPLIQUÉ SAMPLER – 63½" x 75".
Machine appliquéd, pieced, and quilted by the author.

MACHINE APPLIQUÉ: A Sampler of Techniques

Sue Nickels

PATTERNS

This sampler quilt is made up of 12 different blocks, and their designs were inspired by antique folk art quilts. Heart and Hand, the center block from the quilt WITH A LOVING TOUCH, is included on page 102 as a bonus pattern. The designs on these 13 blocks are intermediate to advanced levels. The have complex, multiple pieces per block. The raw-edge fusible method is used for all the blocks in the quilt. Using the raw-edge fusible method makes it possible to create intricate blocks.

A 10" finished-size background block is used. The symmetrical patterns are shown actual size, divided in half. To make a full-size pattern, use a 10" square of tracing paper. With a permanent pen, trace the first half of the pattern. Fold the tracing paper in half and trace the second half from the drawn first half. For the Rose Wreath and Rosebud Wreath patterns, trace the first half of the pattern, then turn the tracing paper to complete the second half, using the leaves as alignment guidelines. The remaining two patterns (Bird in the Garden and Spiral Rose) are asymmetrical and complete patterns are provided. Trace the right half of the pattern. Next, align the broken lines and trace the left half to complete the full-size drawing.

Using the full-size patterns, trace the appliqué pattern pieces directly on the fusible web. If using a pattern that is asymmetrical, the appliqué patterns need to be traced from the reverse. Follow the directions for the raw-edge fusible method to finish the block. Indicate on the pattern when one piece lies underneath another with double slash lines. A straight-stitch

bias-strip is used for many of the stems on these blocks. Special considerations are mentioned with each block.

Directions for completing this sampler quilt are included. Other options may be used to make your own original quilt. Look in the Gallery, page 103, for inspiration.

FOLK GARDEN
APPLIQUÉ PATTERNS

1. Floral Bouquet
2. Crossed Tulips
3. Folk Garden Basket
4. Folk Garden Rose of Sharon
5. Folk Garden Oak Leaves
6. Folk Garden Rose Tree
7. Folk Garden Rose Wreath
8. Heart Wreath
9. Rose Bud Wreath
10. Spiral Rose
11. Spiral Flower Basket
12. Bird in the Garden
13. Bonus Pattern: Heart and Hand

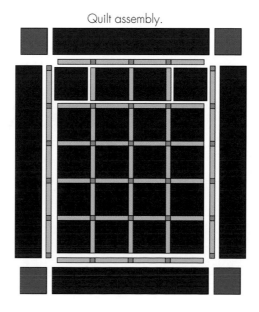

Quilt assembly.

INSTRUCTIONS

Finished quilt size: 63½" x 75"
Finished block size: 10" x 10"

Use 20 appliquéd blocks for the sampler, repeating blocks of your choice. Start with a 12" x 12" background square and rotary cut to 10½" x 10½" after appliquéing the blocks.

YARDAGE

Background blocks	1¾ yards
Appliqué pieces	small amounts of a variety of fabric (total of 3 yards)
Sashing	1 yard
Cornerstones	½ yard
Outer border	2 yards
Corner blocks	¼ yard
Batting	67½" x 79"
Backing	4 yards
Binding	¾ yard
	(for 2½" straight-grain binding)

PREPARATION OF SASHING SEGMENTS

- Cut forty-nine 2" x 10½" strips from the sashing fabric.
- Cut thirty 2" x 2" squares from cornerstone fabric.

CONSTRUCTION OF QUILT TOP

Place the 20 appliquéd blocks in a pleasing arrangement. Sew the appliqué blocks to the sashing strips in rows (Fig. 3–9). Press seams toward sashing strips.

Sew the sashing strips to the cornerstone squares in a row (Fig. 3–10). Press seams toward sashing strips.

Fig. 3–9. Sew appliqué blocks to sashing strips.

Fig. 3–10. Sew sashing strips to cornerstone squares.

Sew the appliqué rows to the sashing rows, referring to the assembly diagram of the quilt on page 87.

CONSTRUCTION OF OUTER BORDER

Cut four 8½" strips from the length of the border fabric. Measure across the center of the quilt for accurate size. Cut borders the correct width and length. Sew top and bottom borders.

Cut four 8½" squares from the corner fabric. Add these to the ends of the remaining borders. Sew side borders to the complete quilt top. Press seams toward borders.

Layer with batting and backing. Baste and quilt as desired. Bind to finish.

Close-up of FOLK GARDEN APPLIQUÉ SAMPLER Folk Garden Rose of Sharon block.

Double slash lines
indicate when an appliqué
piece lies underneath another.

Floral Bouquet

Crossed Tulips

Double slash lines indicate when an appliqué piece lies underneath another.

Folk Garden Basket

Folk Garden
Rose of Sharon

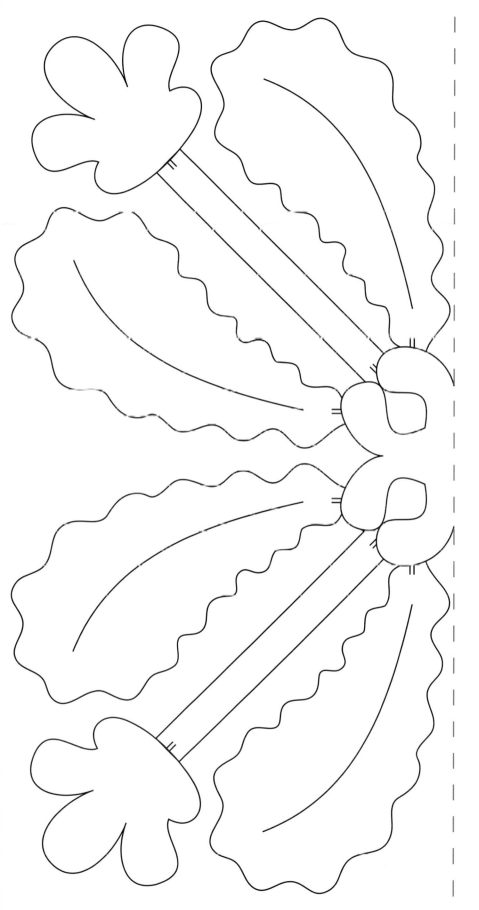

Folk Garden
Oak Leaves

Use stitching for curved
lines in oak leaves.

Double slash lines
indicate when an appliqué
piece lies underneath another.

Double slash lines indicate when an appliqué piece lies underneath another.

Folk Garden Rose Tree

Folk Garden
Rose Wreath

Heart Wreath

Double slash lines indicate when an appliqué piece lies underneath another.

Rose Bud Wreath

Spiral Rose

(2-page pattern)

Sue Nickels

Spiral Rose

(2-page pattern)

Double slash lines
indicate when an appliqué
piece lies underneath another.

Spiral Flower Basket

(trace center flower once)

Double slash lines
indicate when an appliqué
piece lies underneath another.

Use this guide when tracing the cross in the stem.

Bird in the Garden

(trace bird once; trace left side of pattern by folding paper and tracing from drawn right half)

Heart and Hand

Bonus Pattern: Center block from
cover quilt WITH A LOVING TOUCH.

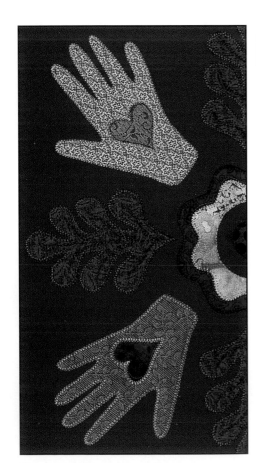

Close-up of WITH A LOVING TOUCH,
Heart and Hand block by the author.

Gallery

OLD HONEY ROSE – 37½" x 37½". Machine pieced, appliquéd, and quilted by Pat Holly, Muskegon, Michigan. This quilt was made with the CLASSIC APPLIQUÉ SAMPLER pattern Roses, Roses, Roses. Pat repeated this design four times using interesting color combinations. A portion of the leaf pattern was used in this clever border for a unique effect. It was stitched using the raw-edge fusible appliqué method.

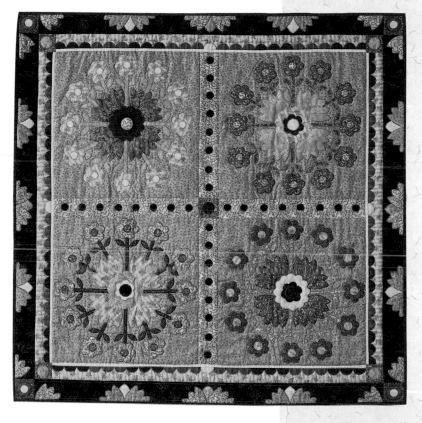

SPRING'S ETERNAL – 50" x 50". Machine appliquéd and quilted by Barb Kilbourn, Ann Arbor, Michigan. Barb's quilt was created using batik fabrics to interpret the FOLK GARDEN APPLIQUÉ SAMPLER patterns. She enlarged the Folk Garden Basket block by 130% and used it as a center medallion, adding some extra flowers. The center is surrounded by eight FOLK GARDEN APPLIQUÉ SAMPLER patterns. It was stitched using the raw-edge fusible method.

SUMMER BOUQUET – 50" x 50".
Machine appliquéd and quilted by Ruth LaCoe, Ann Arbor, Michigan. Ruth used the Cottonball Rose pattern from the SIMPLE APPLIQUÉ SAMPLER. It was repeated four times in each block to form a crossed rose design. These blocks were then set together as a four-block quilt with an original border. Ruth used the raw-edge fusible method to machine appliqué.

WILD ROSES IN THE WOODS
– 41" x 41".
Machine pieced, appliquéd, and quilted by Carol Spaly, Ann Arbor, Michigan. Carol used the Rose Tree pattern from the CLASSIC APPLIQUÉ SAMPLER. The Rose Tree is used as a center medallion and surrounded with a border of leaves and berries. Carol used the template and starch method to machine appliqué.

TULIP SUNDAE – 15" x 21".
Machine appliquéd and quilted by the author. This small quilt contains the Tulip and Heart pattern from the SIMPLE APPLIQUÉ SAMPLER in a unique setting. It was stitched using the raw-edge fusible appliqué method.

BLUE GARDEN – 26" x 36".
Machine appliquéd and quilted by Sue Holdaway-Heys, Ann Arbor, Michigan. The Cottonball Rose pattern from the SIMPLE APPLIQUÉ SAMPLER was used in this small quilt. Sue used hand-painted fabrics, a watercolor pencil, and free-motion surface stitching to create this unique, contemporary version of a traditional block. Sue used the raw-edge fusible method.

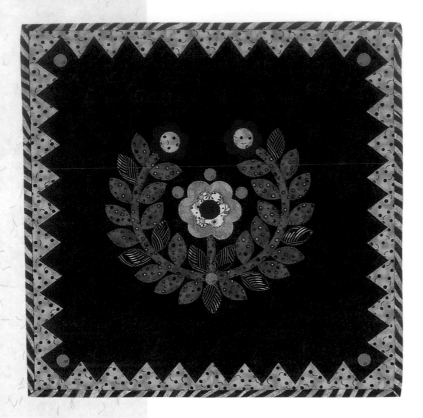

FOLK GARDEN ROSE TREE AND **FOLK GARDEN ROSE OF SHARON** – 18" x 18" each.
Machine appliquéd and quilted by the author. These one-block quilts were made using the Folk Garden patterns they are named for. They were stitched with the raw-edge fusible appliqué method. This is a nice way to learn the method and complete a small project, too.

SPRING'S HERALD – 43" x 43".
Machine pieced, appliquéd, and quilted by Mary Ann Fielder, Manchester, Michigan. Two patterns from the CLASSIC APPLIQUÉ SAMPLER were used in this wall quilt. The Rose of Sharon is surrounded by four Fancy Wreaths in this clever set. Mary Ann also added flower and leaf segments along the border. The raw-edge fusible method was used for these appliqué blocks.

HOPSCOTCH AND COTTON CANDY – 43" x 43".
Machine pieced, appliquéd, and hand quilted by Nancy Chizek, Ann Arbor, Michigan. Nancy used the Folk Garden Rose of Sharon pattern as a center medallion. The leaf and flower unit from the pattern was used to create an original border. The raw-edge fusible method was used for the appliqué blocks.

Blue Tulips on Pink Skies – 76" x 81".

Machine appliquéd and quilted by the author. This quilt was inspired by Amish Bar quilts. Appliquéd flowers and vines adorn the alternating bars, and the quilting reflects an Amish style. The raw-edge fusible method was used on this quilt.

WITH A LOVING TOUCH – 43" x 43".
Machine pieced, appliquéd, and quilted by the author. This quilt was made for an exhibit by Paradigm Quilters called Women's Work. It was stitched using the raw-edge fusible method.

Recommended Reading

Anderson, Faye. *Appliqué Designs – My Mother Taught Me To Sew,* AQS, 1990.

Fanning, Robbie and Tony. *The Complete Book of Machine Quilting,* Chilton Book Company, 1980.

Hargrave, Harriet. *Mastering Machine Appliqué,* C&T Publishing, 1991.

Marston, Gwen and Joe Cunningham. *American Beauties: Rose & Tulip Quilts,* AQS, 1988.

Martin, Letty. *Straight Stitch Machine Appliqué,* AQS, 1994.

Wagner, Debra. *Traditional Quilts – Today's Techniques,* Krause Publications, 1997.

Sources

I have researched these products and am confident of the success achieved with them. There are other products that work well, but these are the ones I have found work the best with the techniques being used. Most of the products are easily available at quilt shops. I like to support my local quilt shops as they are working hard to provide quilters with the best products on the market.

COTTON THREAD (30-WEIGHT): Madeira Tanne (Can be used for a heavier decorative look.)

COTTON THREAD (50-WEIGHT): Mettler Silk Finish and Madeira Tanne (These threads come in a wide range of colors.)

COTTON THREAD (60-WEIGHT): Mettler Embroidery

HEAT-RESISTANT TEMPLATE PLASTIC: Templar (It is easy to draw on, very heat resistant, and reusable.)

PENCIL: Quilter's Choice fabric marking pencil

SELF-THREADING NEEDLE: EZ brand

SEWING MACHINE: Bernina 170 QE (It has a great blanket stitch and all of the wonderful machine accessories listed in the Supplies section.)

SEWING MACHINE NEEDLES: Schmetz Universal

SPRAY STARCH: Niagara aerosol (regular)

TRANSPARENT NYLON THREAD: YLI .004 weight

About the Author

Sue Nickels has taught machine quilting and appliqué techniques for ten years. She has made quilts for over 20 years, starting with hand techniques and gradually focusing on machine work. A regular teacher at The Icehouse in Grayling, Michigan, she has also taught and lectured at American Quilter's Society (AQS), National Quilting Association, and International Quilt Association shows. Sue has taught at national conferences including the Empty Spools Seminar at Asilomar and Quilting-by-the-Sound in Washington, internationally in England, and she is a much-sought instructor in guilds across the country.

Co-author of two books with her sister, Pat Holly, the sisters also sew quilts together. Their quilt, BLACKBIRDS FLY, won many national awards, and THE BEATLES QUILT claimed the 1998 AQS Best of Show award.

Sue's quilts have appeared in numerous publications. TURKEY TEARS appeared in the November 1998 issue of *Quilter's Newsletter Magazine*. LE PANIER DE FLEURS was awarded First Place Wall Quilt at the 2000 Quilter's Heritage Celebration in Lancaster and also won third place quilt in the AQS 2000 Quilt Exhibition in Nashville, Tennessee. Sue has also designed a line of quilting stencils for machine quilting available through Quilting Creations International, Inc.

She lives in Ann Arbor, Michigan, with her husband, Tim, and two daughters, Jessica and Ashley. Jessica is a graduate architecture student at the University of Virginia in Charlottesville. Ashley is an undergraduate student at the University of Michigan in Ann Arbor.

Her priorities are to make the best quilts she can using today's technology and to share her knowledge with quilters everywhere.

Other AQS Books

This is only a small selection of the books available from the American Quilter's Society. AQS books are known worldwide for timely topics, clear writing, beautiful color photos, and accurate illustrations and patterns. The following books are available from your local bookseller, quilt shop, or public library.

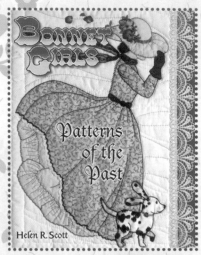

#5763 US$21.95

#5845 US$21.95

#5338 US$21.95

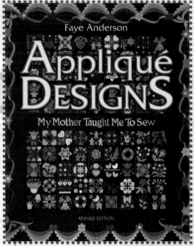

#5760 US$18.95

#5851 US$18.95

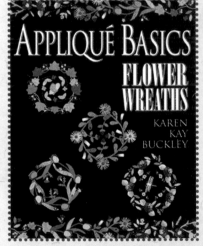

#5335 US$21.95

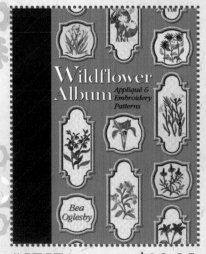

#5757 US$19.95

#5794 US$16.95

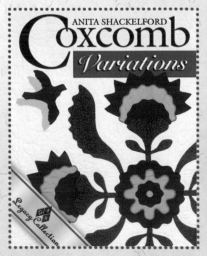

#5706 US$18.95

LOOK FOR THESE BOOKS NATIONALLY OR CALL 1-800-626-5420